WORKSHOPS IN COMPUTING
Series edited by C. J. van Rijsbergen

W0246233

Also in this series

Liesbeth Dusink and Patrick Hall (Eds.)

Software Re-use, Utrecht 1989

Proceedings of the Software Re-use Workshop,
23–24 November 1989,
Utrecht, The Netherlands

Springer-Verlag Berlin Heidelberg GmbH

Liesbeth M. Dusink, PhD
Delft University of Technology
PO Box 356
2600 AJ Delft
The Netherlands

Patrick A. V. Hall, PhD
Department of Computer Science
Brunel University
Uxbridge
Middlesex UB8 3PH, UK

ISBN 978-3-540-19652-5

British Library Cataloguing in Publication Data
Software Re-use
Software re-use, Utrecht 1989.
1. Word processing. Use of microcomputers. Software
I. Title II. Dusink, Liesbeth 1957– III. Hall, Patrick A. V. IV. British Computer
Society V. Series
652.55369
ISBN 978-3-540-19652-5
Library of Congress Cataloging-in-Publication Data
Software Re-use Workshop (1989: Utrecht, Netherlands)
Software re-use, Utrecht 1989: Proceedings of the Software Re-use
Workshop. 23–24 November 1989. Utrecht, The Netherlands/ Liesbeth Dusink
and Patrick Hall, eds.
p. cm. — (Workshops in computing)
Published in collaboration with the British Computer Society.
Includes bibliographical references and index.
ISBN 978-3-540-19652-5   ISBN 978-1-4471-3536-4 (eBook)
DOI 10.1007/978-1-4471-3536-4
1. Computer software—Reusability—Congresses. I. Dusink, Liesbeth, 1957–
  II. Hall, Patrick A.V. III. British Computer Society. IV. Title. V. Series.
QA76.76.R47S66 1991   91-10595
005—dc20   CIP

Apart from any fair dealing for the purposes of research or private study, or
criticism or review, as permitted under the Copyright, Designs and Patents Act
1988, this publication may only be reproduced, stored or transmitted, in any
form, or by any means, with the prior permission in writing of the publishers, or
in the case of reprographic reproduction in accordance with the terms of
licences issued by the Copyright Licensing Agency. Enquiries concerning
reproduction outside those terms should be sent to the publishers.

© Springer-Verlag Berlin Heidelberg 1991
Originally published by Springer-Verlag Berlin Heidelberg New York 1991

The use of registered names, trademarks etc. in this publication does not imply,
even in the absence of a specific statement, that such names are exempt from
the relevant laws and regulations and therefore free for general use.

34/3830–543210 Printed on acid-free paper

Preface

In November 1989 we organised a workshop on software re-use, inviting members of the leading research teams across Europe. In retrospect, we realise that we missed a few research teams out, but nevertheless we did have a very fruitful workshop. This book is the outcome of that meeting.

Prior to the workshop, teams submitted short position papers, and at the workshop made very short presentations of these. Most of the time was spent in four parallel sessions, and the reports of these sessions are given in Chapter 2. After the workshop we invited the attendees to revise and resubmit their papers in the light of the workshop, and it is these updated papers that appear in Chapter 4 onwards. The papers are in alphabetical order of first author.

To complete this text we have added an introduction to software re-use as a first chapter – this was prepared by Liesbeth Dusink. We have added a comprehensive bibliography as Chapter 3, merging the bibliographies accumulated at Delft and at Brunel.

To be able to organise the workshop we were sponsored by SERC, the Software Engineering Research Centre in Utrecht, Netherlands.

November 1990   Liesbeth Dusink
                                                      Pat Hall

Contents

List of Contributors

Cornelia Boldyreff
Department of Computer Science, Brunel University, Uxbridge,
Middlesex UB8 3PH, U.K.
tel. (0895) 74000 x 2399

P.T. Breuer
Programming Research Group, Oxford University,
8–11 Keble Road, Oxford OX1 3QD, U.K.
tel. (0865) 273840
e-mail: ..!uunet!mcvax!ukc!ox-prg!ptb

C. Bron
University of Groningen, Faculteit der Wiskunde en
Natuurwetenschappen, Wiskunde en Informatica, Landleven 5,
postbus 800, 9700 AV Groningen, The Netherlands
+31(50)633926

Joachim Cramer
Software Technology Center, Helenenbergweg 19,
D-4600 Dortmund 50, Germany

E.J. Dijkstra
University of Groningen, Faculteit der Wiskunde en
Natuurwetenschappen, Wiskunde en Informatica, Landleven 5,
postbus 800, 9700 AV Groningen, The Netherlands
+31(50)633926

Ernst-Erich Doberkat
Informatik/Software Engineering, Department of Mathematics,
University of Essen, Schützenbahn 70, D-4300 Essen 1, Germany
uucp: .../mcvax/unido/unieinf/eed

E.M. Dusink
Delft University of Technology, P.O. Box 356, 2600 AJ Delft,
The Netherlands
e-mail: betje@dutiaa.tudelft.nl

Ulrich Gutenbeil
Informatik/Software Engineering, Department of Mathematics,
University of Essen, Schützenbahn 70, D-4300 Essen 1,
Germany
uucp: .../mcvax/unido/unieinf/eed

Pat Hall
Department of Computer Science, Brunel University, Uxbridge,
Middlesex UB8 3PH, U.K.
tel. (0895) 74000 x 2399

E. Hochmüller
Institut für Informatik, Universität Klagenfurt, A 9022 Klagenfurt,
Austria
e-mail: rossak@edvz.uni-klagenfurt.ada.at

Heike Huennekens
Software Technology Center, Helenenbergweg 19,
D-4600 Dortmund 50, Germany

K. Lano
Programming Research Group, Oxford University,
8–11 Keble Road, Oxford OX1 3QD, U.K.
tel. 0865 273840
e-mail: ..!uunet!mcvax!ukc!ox-prg!lano

Neil Maiden
Department of Business Systems Analysis, City University,
Northampton Square, London EC1V 0HB, U.K.
tel: +44 1 253 4399 x 3420
e-mail: sf328@uk.ac.city (JANET)

O.Univ.-Prof.Dipl.-Ing.Mag.Dr. Roland Mittermeir
Institut für Informatik, Univesität für Bildungswissenschaften
Klagenfurt, Universitätsstrasse 65-67, A-9022 Klagenfurt, Austria
tel. (463) 5317 575
e-mail: mittermeir@edvz.uni-klagenfurt.ada.at

W. Rossak
Institut für Informatik, Universität Klagenfurt, A 9022 Klagenfurt,
Austria
e-mail: rossak@edvz.uni-klagenfurt.ada.at

Wilhelm Schaefer
Software Technolgy Center, Helenenbergweg 19,
D-4600 Dortmund 50, Germany

K. Sikkel
Software Engineering Research Centrum, Lauge Viestraat 365,
3511 BK Utrecht, The Netherlands

Alistair Sutcliffe
Department of Business Systems Analysis, City University,
Northampton Square, London EC1V 0HB, U.K.
tel: +44 1 253 4399 x 3420
e-mail: sf328@uk.ac.city (JANET)

J.C. van Vliet
Vrije Universiteit, Amsterdam, The Netherlands
Faculteit Wiskunde en Informatica, Department of Mathematics
and Computer Science, De Boelelaan 1081, 1081 HV Amsterdam,
Nederland
tel. +31 (20)548 8080
e-mail: postbox@cs.vu.nl

Dr. Martin Ward
Computer Science Department, Science Labs, South Road,
Durham DH1 3LE, U.K.
e-mail: ...!mcvax!ukc!easby!martin

Stefan Wolf
Software Technology Center, Helenenbergweg 19,
D-4600 Dortmund 50, Germany

Jian Zhang
Department of Computer Science, Brunel University, Uxbridge,
Middlesex UB8 3PH, U.K.
tel. (0895) 74000 x 2399

Chapter 1

Introduction to Re-use

Although the term *software crisis* is an old one (McIllroy 1976), the problem it describes is still real. The term expresses a discrepancy between the demand for large complex software systems and the ability to build such systems. Existing solutions to the problem are higher level languages and the usage of tools. These solutions, however, only partially solve the problem. Other ideas, such as automating the production process and the usage of existing (software) parts, are only applied in very restricted domains.

Those last two ideas are covered with the term *re-use*, although the form of re-use differs. Without any further definition of the term *re-use* every call of a program is re-use of a program. We'll be more precise and give the following definition: Re-use is considered as a means to support the construction of *new programs* using in a systematical way existing designs, design fragments, program texts, documentation, or other forms of program representation. This excludes porting and maintenance because these activities are based on keeping the same software in a changing (hard- or software) environment.

For the automation of the production process, parts (components) have to exist. Components represent solutions to problems encountered formerly. Such components might represent solutions for design problems, architectural problems, or coding problems. They can be bound to a specific application domain, and implement certain functions and operations in that domain (virtual machines for a given domain) a typical example being a package for terminal I/O, while other components are more general computing or transforming devices (connection-components), parameterised on input, function and output (a typical example being a queue or a stack). These parts, whether or not automatically used, can be re-used in two ways: transformational and compositional.

- In the *transformational* approach programs are written in terms of abstract specifications using a wide-spectrum language (ie. a language with both components from very high-level languages and components from low-level languages). These languages are domain specific. The abstract specifications are transformed automatically into efficient target programs using domain knowledge in the transformation rules and using existing components.

- In the *compositional* approach (the software IC approach) software components, eg. packages, functions and other forms of modules, are used as basic building blocks in the software construction process. Programs are constructed by combining existing software components (either in source form or some other representation form). A special language (component composition language) can be used to combine the components together to form new programs

(Prieto-Diaz 1986).

In both approaches software and/or designs are re-used, the important difference between the approaches is the way components are re-used, while furthermore the way new software is constructed is different. However, they can clearly be combined.

By re-using components, gain is made in several ways. During design and implementation less errors occur, mainly because proven components can be used. Furthermore, the software is delivered faster, since development does not start from scratch. Finally, less errors are made, since the complexity is hidden within the components and does not have to show to the user.

It must be realised that, by current practice, the coding process consumes approximately 13% of the resources in the software development process. Although the contribution of even the simplest forms of code re-use may contribute to savings in other parts of the life cycle as well (in particular to corrective maintenance), this contribution is not very well established as yet. Obviously, in the long run, effectiveness of software re-use may increase when it is applied to more phases of the development process.

1.1   THE TRANSFORMATIONAL APPROACH

The transformational approach can be categorised as *automatic programming*. The programmer *programs* in terms of very high-level abstract algorithms written in some wide-spectrum language, using domain-oriented specifications. A support system, probably an assistant-type system, interprets the algorithms or specifications and executes them directly or it locates pieces of program in the database that (partially) satisfy the specification. In this last case, the support system then translates the abstract specifications into an efficient program in some executable language. The support system always has access to a library of predefined transformation schemes. In order for the approach to be practically useful, the support system should provide a high-degree of mechanical support in performing program transformation of specifications and abstract algorithms to efficient target programs.

This approach is also known as a *wide-spectrum approach to software re-use* (Cheatham 1984). Knowledge of the application domains is used in the language itself as well as in the transformation rules.

The transformational approach is strongly advocated as a mechanism for the foundation of the envisioned software factory (MacAnAirchinnigh 1987). The desirability of this approach and advances in this area are addressed by various authors and organisations, eg. Neighbors 1984. Practical applications of the approach, however, strongly depend on areas of computer science in which more research is required before the results are practically applicable (in particular areas like program transformation techniques with or without AI). It depends also on the domain for which the software has to be written. If it is a well known, stable domain a wide-spectrum language can be constructed, otherwise this approach can not be used. The current degree of practicability of the approach is limited to small application domains which are very well known, eg. parser generators. As the topic of the workshop was component-based re-use, this direction of re-usability will not be pursued in this chapter.

1.2 THE COMPOSITIONAL APPROACH

In the compositional approach the engineer, the programmer, searches for and combines (instances of) pre-fabricated components, ie. existing program modules, to form larger components or programs. The algorithms and specifications have to be understood and used by the programmer. He has to select the components and has to chose and perform the transformations.

The support for combining components can be automatic instantiation of generics, type conversions, tailoring, and the like. By automatic parameterisation and automatic tailoring of components the difference between the compositional approach and the transformational approach rapidly disappears.

Within the compositional approach re-use can be applied as black box, glass box and as white box re-use. If the black box method is used, only the interface of the component and a specification is available, with glass box also the contents of the components can be seen but not touched, and with white box the components can also be tailored. This tailoring can be done with help of an editor, or parts of the implementation are overridden by new code in a manner similar to that used in frames (eg. Bassett 1987).

In the ideal case the programmer has knowledge of the application domain, a filled components library, components which can be treated as you like, a design method which stimulates re-use, a coherent set of tools, quality assurance, and measurement techniques.

1.3 QUESTIONS ABOUT RE-USE

The study of components-based re-use can be divided into several topics. These topics are: acquisition of components, storage/retrieval of components, usage of components and metrics on components. During the workshop two groups discussed the acquisition of components and one group discussed the usage of components. The storage of components and the metrics were not discussed as separate topics. In this section they are dealt with in their own right as they have problems outside the scope of re-use.

1.3.1 Acquisition of Components

The first thing to be done to be able to apply re-use is to acquire components. Acquisition of components can be done in two ways. One way is to develop components from scratch and the other way is to extract components out of existing software. Quite some research concentrates on how to develop re-usable components at code level. This research results mostly in guidelines about the naming of identifiers, the number and type of parameters and the dependencies on the environment (Bott et al. 1986, Burton et al. 1987, Gargaro 1987). A few people extract components out of existing software, a form of reverse engineering.

As with most things, we can ask ourselves *what* and *how*. What components do we need and how should they look like. An answer to the first question, the what, can only be given after domain analysis. The resulting description of the domain contains knowledge in the form of semantic nets, in which principles, relations, uncertainties, terminology, etc. are described. As most domains are less mature than physics there will be more hypotheses and gaps.

An answer to the second question, the how, will be a combined answer of the following questions:

- How can you give a description of the functionality and the operation of components and their parameters which is easy to write and to grasp? What kind of guidelines are possible to guide the specification of software components?

- What are the external features of the components, such as the connection among the elements in the interface, the amount of parameterisation, and the possibilities of tailoring? Parameterisation is a controversial topic. On the one hand it is needed to make a component more general (and thus, according to many people, more re-usable), on the other hand, a high degree of parameterisation may make it less understandable and usable.

- What is an appropriate scale for components? Literature suggests that re-using larger components is more profitable, since the larger the component, the bigger the profit once it is re-used (Ratcliffe 1987). On the other hand, the functionality of a large component is often such that the number of times it actually can be re-used is small. Smaller components are used more frequently but the profit for each time the component is re-used is smaller.

- Is it possible to develop generic designs for domains? Is it possible to derive guidelines for the implementation of components?

- When is it useful to build general connection components, eg. a generalised data structure?

- Is it possible to specify guidelines and procedures to adapt components to fulfill certain needs?

- To what extent is it possible to extract components from existing software.

- What do components look like on higher abstraction levels then code?

1.3.2 Storage/Retrieval of Components

Some form of software component library must be available, for the storage of components (and their descriptions) and to allow forms of browsing and querying. The existence of a library introduces problems with entering components into the library eg. methods and techniques for classification and description, retrieving components from the library and managing the library.

The method of component storage and retrieval heavily depends on the envisaged use of such components. Some research concentrates on the topic of storage without considering the use of the storage and the use of the components.

Components have to be stored in such a way that they can be found and retrieved whenever needed. The questions are (again what and how) what to store and how to store it. As components libraries can be seen as normal libraries, knowledge about libraries can be used to answer parts of the questions.

As to how to store, techniques from data bases can be used. Prieto-Diaz 1987 and Burton et al. 1987 designed and implemented systems adapted for re-use. For example, they worked with fuzzy logic. This topic is fairly established, techniques exist and work, research can be done on special retrieval languages/specification languages, matching specifications (automatic deduction that two formal specifications mean the same).

Prieto-Diaz suggests ways of storing and retrieving components, although they restrict themselves to procedural-oriented components at code level. Other research is done in AI, mainly oriented towards research in which various kinds of *assistants* are developed, eg. Arthur 1986, Bassett 1987, and Conradi 1987.

1.3.3   Usage of Components

Little research has been done on the usage of components. We think that this topic is essential, as without the usage of components no re-use will be applied and the acquisition and storage of components is wasted. In spite of the availability of large libraries with code components, systematic re-use has not yet been shown. The two most important problems are the lacking of a design method based on the re-use philosophy and the integration of components into a coherent working system.

If re-use is applied it is often an ad hoc process done on an individual basis and as an afterthought. This process should be turned into a systematic way of working on corporate wide level. This means that a design method has to be developed which is based on a re-use philosophy and which stimulates re-use in the whole development process. Furthermore, to kill two birds with one stone, the method should not exclude the re-use of existing software, and should deliver re-usable components as a by-product of the design method as well.

Domain analysis will play an important role in such a design method to be able to get designs where the parts do match with existing components. A components library with its retrieval system will play an important role too, to find (nearly) matching components.

A problem with the usage of components is their integration, together with each other and with other software. The connection problem can be divided into two subproblems. One subproblem is the actual connection between interfaces that do not match exactly, ie. how can interfaces be converted such that they match. The other subproblem deals with configurations. Is it possible to have a configuration description language which describes the extraction of the right components (possibly from some library and transforming it into some appropriate format) and their connection, like a somewhat more sophisticated MAKE program. Prieto-Diaz 1986 describes a module interconnection language and Neighbors 1984 decsribes the DRACO approach.

1.3.4   Metrics

Metrics may play an important role in quality assurance, especially in the acquisition of components and in deciding whether they should be used or not. Metrics should provide a basis for deciding whether re-use is sensible, whether it is cost-effective to adapt an existing component or to build a component from scratch. In short, metrics which address cost savings on component basis are needed. Metrics can be seen as part of the topics acquisition and usage. We mention it separately, just because the topic appears in several other ones.

Questions we should like to have answered are:

- Is it possible to determine metrics to measure the degree of re-usability for specific applications and application domains; if yes, how should it be measured?

- Is it possible to establish the quality of components; if yes, how should it be established?

- Is it possible to measure the cost of adapting a component; if yes, how should it be measured?

- In which cases is it wise to build components from scratch?

- When is it useful to specify and implement a virtual machine for a specific application domain?

- When is it useful to implement components by adapting existing ones?

As even metrics to establish the costs of the development of a new software system are not very reliable, we still have a long way to go.

Chapter 2

Workshop Overview and Conclusions

2.1 GENERAL VIEW OF SOFTWARE RE-USE

The area of software re-use can be viewed as comprising four parts, as shown in figure 2.1

- domain analysis

- development with re-use

- design for re-use

- reverse engineering

The last two of these are the methods by which we obtain re-usable components, and have together been called

- component engineering.

Component Engineering is concerned with the production of components suitable for re-use. Components can either be newly built in a process called here **design for re-use,** as has been done for Ada (eg. Booch 1987), or they could be retrieved from existing code using **reverse engineering,** as is being done on the Practitioner project (eg. Boldyreff et al. 1990). These will need to be produced in conformance to particular standards. Design for Re-use is primarily concerned with these standards, with models of components and their interconnection, with the way components can be parameterised to make them more re-usable, and with more general concerns for the quality and robustness of the components. Reverse engineering is concerned with the extraction of components from existing software, through the analysis of both code and documentation, possibly helped by software engineers, abstracting and generalising these so that they become widely re-usable.

These components need to be useful, to relate to real needs — these real needs will be discovered through **domain analysis** which, for a particular application domain, will identify possible components ("concepts") and principles concerning how they might be put together. In the limit this knowledge about a domain may be manifest as a domain specific language, but it need not necessarily take this form. For example, domain analysis could just recommend particular components for interconnection using some standard module interconnection language, see Prieto-Diaz 1986 and Neighbours 1986.

8

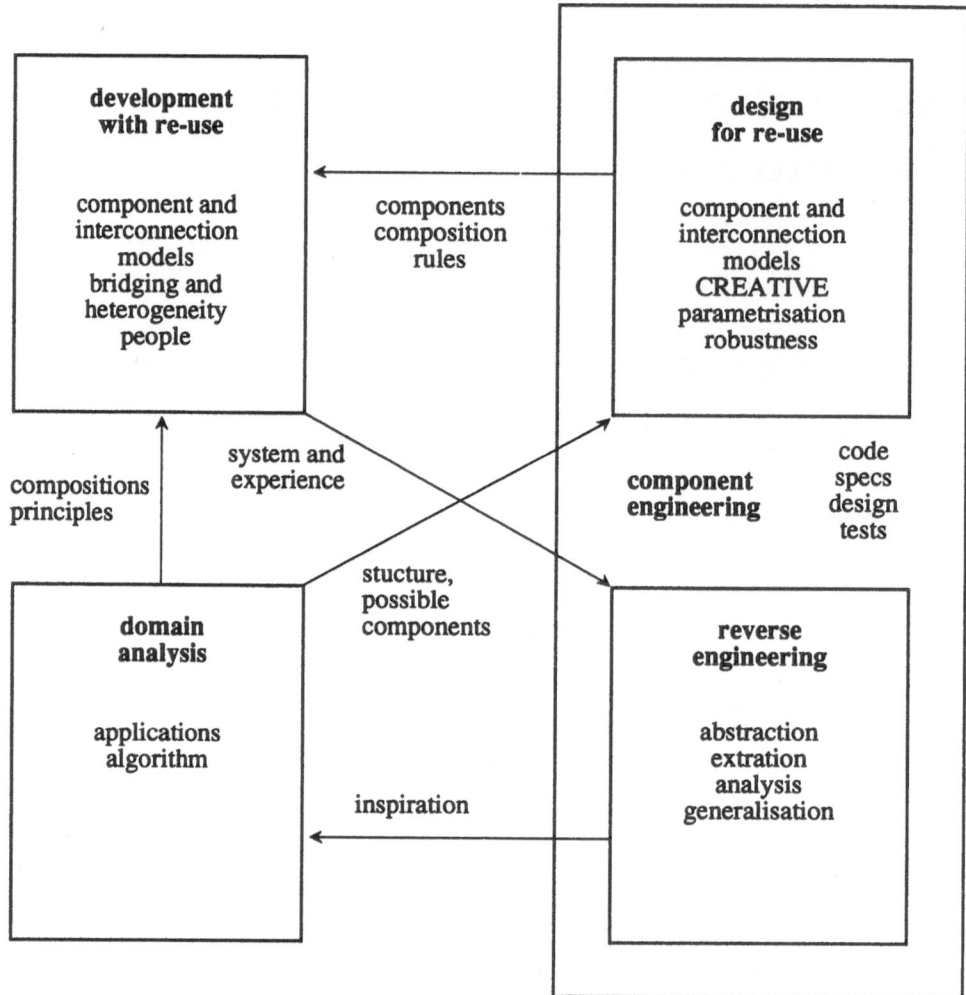

Figure 2.1 Decomposition of Software Re-use into four inter-related areas.

Development methods have almost all been produced for the development of new software — the whole process of **development with re-use** needs to be addressed. The re-use of existing components may constrain software development — but also help it. Standard designs for particular domains may be used (just higher level components). Components which only partly meet the requirements may need to be used, with extra software added to produce the complete system.

These four areas were the subject of the working groups, and the reports of these groups are set out below.

2.2 DOMAIN ANALYSIS

Abstract of the discussion on domain analysis during the reuse workshop, SERC, Utrecht, the Netherlands, 23-24 November 1989
Participants to the discussion: L. Dusink (reporter), R. Gautier, J. Mariani, D. Mole, H. van Vliet

Domain analysis (DA), the process of analyzing what concepts exist on a certain knowledge domain, is, as such, not intrinsically a software engineering topic, but DA is relevant to software engineering insofar as it enables us to build better software. It helps us to achieve the right levels of abstraction in software products. The knowledge gained during the process of DA is all persuasive in the software development process, whether or not oriented towards re-use.

We consider the process of DA as a creative one which has to be performed by an expert in the domain who is capable of producing usable products with, for example, the technique of reverse engineering. Although the process is very interesting and should be attended to, we found ourselves unable to say much more about the process. Therefor, we will concentrate on the products of DA in this paper.

The primary product of DA is a language for describing objects in the domain. The language defines the domain. It is to a large extent up to the domain analyst to define the boundaries of the domain being analyzed. The domain language that results from a domain analysis is an attempt at a language which can describe all objects in the domain as recognised by the domain analyst(s). Once that language has been defined, however, from the point of view of the users of the language, the domain **is** the set of objects which can be described by that language. The language embodies concepts relevant to the domain (both domain specific and non domain specific as eg. mathematics). The language should be on an intermediate level between problem space and underlying machine and should have two interfaces, in this case definitions, a user-oriented one and an implementor-oriented one. The user-oriented definition is in terms the users need to know or are familiar with. The implementor-oriented definition is in terms of other domain languages and component specifications. See figure 2.2 with the concepts on level A as the user interface and the concepts on level B as the implementor interface.

Of course, these two definitions should be consistent and need not involve a concrete syntax.

Domain languages will develop gradually. In immature domains only vocabulary, components and interconnection semantics will be found with hardly the possibility of forming these into a language. In the immature domains, component-based re-use is the base on which the domain language will be built. In mature domains, languages can be defined out of these products. In mature domains, we are likely to have higher level knowledge of how to construct solutions, and will tend to build smarter tools (eg. parser generators). However, this does not preclude the use of components. What happens is that we let tools fit the components together for us, or let them transform the components for us. Thus in mature domains, users will apply no longer component-based re-use but transformation-based re-use.

If the re-use domain is split into four parts: the creation of re-usable components, the abstraction of re-usable components from existing software, the development of software using existing components, and domain analysis, one is able to discriminate

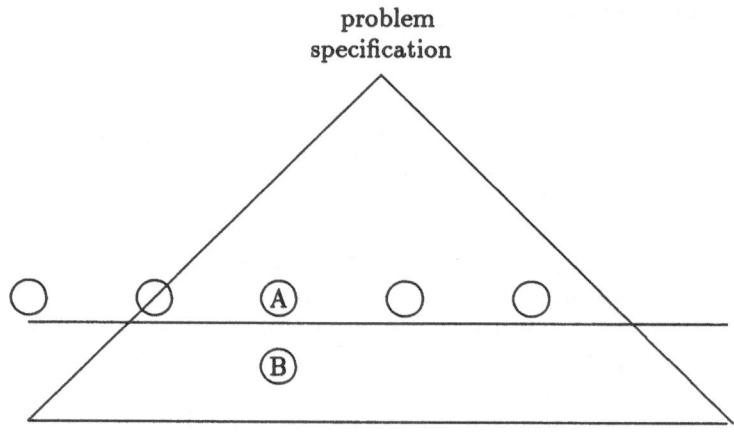

Figure 2.2 From specification to implementation

between the different usages of the products of DA and the different kinds of input from the other parts.

For the creation of components, DA is expected to produce specifications of components and DA imports the description techniques from this part to be used in the implementor-oriented definition. For the abstraction of components, DA is expected to offer inspiration and vocabulary. Inspiration from reverse engineering and techniques for finding concepts are imported from this part. For the development of software using existing components DA provides a domain language, which provides a user-oriented way of describing software which can be built from those components. The domain language will normally be supported by tools which interpret domain language statements to produce software by component interconnection or transformation.

2.3   DESIGN FOR RE-USE

Abstract of the discussion on domain analysis during the reuse workshop, SERC, Utrecht, the Netherlands, 23-24 November 1989
Participants to the discussion: P. Breuer, C. Bron (reporter), T. Bull, E. Doberkat, H.-K. Li, R. Mittermeir (reporter), K. Sikkel, H. Weber

2.3.1   Design for Re-use: Is It Different?

The overall structure of the workshop has been set out in such a way that participants where to attach themselves to either one of the four groups:

- Design with re-use (DwR)

- Design for re-use (DfR)

- Reverse engineering (ReEng)

- Domain analysis (DA)

This division of labour suggests already (— by definition of the other groups) that "Design for Re-use" has to deal with the slightly cynical topic of addressing the re-usability issue from the vantage point of software, which does not yet exist. Hence, by definition, it cannot be re-used right away, but has to be "used" in the normal way first (if at all!).

Thus, the contrast to Design with Re-use (DwR) is obvious in that DwR has to do with finding the right components and glueing them together properly, while Design for Re-use (DfR) is responsible for making components which are readily retrievable (ie. describable) and smooth enough to be easily glued together without much additional effort.

The constraint that they should be readily integrable into a more comprehensive whole demarcates the borderline to Reverse Engineering (ReE). Here — if seen in the context of software re-use — one addresses also the parts or components level. However, one acknowledges the fact that real life software might have been developed (or evolved) under certain constraints which forced edges into it and that those edges are hindering direct re-use. Hence, this software will be subjected to a — hopefully computer supported — process to make it worthy for integration into a new system. Therefore, one might draw the borderline between Reverse Engineering and DfR as one between the scruffies and the neats.

But if DfR deals just with software which is yet to be produced, what makes it different from good design anyway? Is this more than a new catch word for old wisdom?

Most participants in the DfR discussion group felt — no wonder (!) — it is more than that. At least two reasons can be put forward, in favour of this argument:

1. In ordinary design, one designs a component (usually following some top down approach) into its environment.

   With DfR this environment does not yet exist. Hence, the notion of information hiding is essentially reversed. Instead of the rule "Design your components such that they do not rely on internals of their subcomponents", we have to put forward "Design your components such that they do not rely on internals of their future environment".

2. Ordinary design rules require engineers to make their components maintainable and understandable. While maintainability shares certainly important aspects with modifiability and hence with support for partial re-use, understandability can be understood in classical systems as understandability in context.

   Since this context is missing for a component to be re-used, we have

   - to be more careful in terms of its development, documentation and testability

   - to come up with rules for establishing a minimal context for understandability and safe usage.

- to design components that strike a proper balance between "a straight forward, easily understandable interface" on one hand, and "a sufficient degree of parameterisability, to match the component with its future uses (as yet unknown)" on the other hand.

Definitely, one could come up with a longer list of arguments justifying DfR. However, the two issues mentioned above seemed to be the ones most obviously (while implicitly) present in our discussions.

2.3.2 Design for Re-use: for What Kind of Re-use?

Why do people want to re-use software? Because they want to build systems faster and more economical than they do now! These arguments have also been put forward in discussions about software process models, notably in favour of (rapid) prototyping. Hence, we should ask whether re-use has anything to do with rapid prototyping.

Before addressing this issue, we should state that it is now common wisdom, that the term *Software Re-use* does not refer to re-use of executable code only; in fact it does so to an ever lesser extent.

Further, one makes the distinction between total and partial re-use. In the first case, a component is re-used on an as-it-is basis, whereas in the second case, it may be subjected to modifications — hence, for this latter case, DfR would also encompass Design for Modifiability.

The distinction between re-use in systems construction and re-use when developing prototypes, is definitely not a sharp one. It does, however, place severe constraints on the DwR agenda and for DfR it is indication to which extent performance constraints are to be considered or emphasised. It should be noted here, that the development cost of a highly re-usable component has the chance to be distributed over a large number of application systems to be built. Hence, higher emphasis may be placed on various quality items — performance being only one of them.

If, on the other hand, DwR is to be understood as producing rapidly some kind of a system collage (prototype) to give the user a rough idea about what the finally delivered system might be like, we would have less constraints on performance considerations and even less concerns about fully matching functionality.

Since modern software development does recommend an integration between document driven and experiment driven approaches (eg. Spiral model), the above distinction is of diminishing importance. Via evolutionary development, one can take the glued together prototype and enhance it by recarving those portions where potential problems (functionality, performance, ease of use, ...) are surfacing. It should be noted though, that with this kind of evolution, the overall architecture of the application system remains. To which extent this is a potential problem will depend on the size of the system and the percentage of re-used software versus new software as well as on the closeness of re-used software to executable code.

2.3.3   Facets of Design for Re-use

Architectural Level Considerations.

Concern for the architectural level is notably given by the ESF-project, a multi-national, multiorganisational cooperative effort under Eureka sponsorship. Weber presented his view on a uniform module structure for ESF-software. The proposed ESF-modules provide a clear separation between body and interface structure. The latter is suggested to be split into the modules import- and its export-interface as well as a section dealing with so called "common parameters" which are passed through the module as a kind of tramp data.

This module architecture is complemented in ESF by a systems architecture where several server and client modules are located around a (if necessary: structured) software bus. This has of course obvious relationships to DwR.

Obviously, these architectural suggestions came close to suggestions calling for the subsumption of DfR under object oriented design. However, while object-oriented design would satisfy the aesthetical properties needed, it will not be strong enough to make all the non-object-oriented software in the field die soon.

Component Level Considerations.

At this level, in heated debates, two complementary approaches have been presented

1. software normalisation, and

2. software parameterisation.

With software normalisation, as proposed by Mittermeir, rules are given for engineering pieces in such a way, that their integrability into future systems is maximised. These rules are not on the architectural level, but on the level of providing components with clean semantics in much the same way as normalisation in the database field gives formal rules for providing relations with clear semantics. (Having normalised relations on software components does, however, obviously influence the overall architecture of the system.) Similarly to data normalisation, software normalisation does also provide a set of layered normal forms, leading eventually to the highest class of semantic crispness.

Parameterisation of components, as advocated by Bron, attacks the DfR issue from a different angle. Re-usability of components, designed according to the principle of the "good taste" of a programmer, is enhanced by abstracting those parts of the algorithm which might conceivably vary in different applications. The specific variant of a component, which is needed for a particular application will be instantiated in languages like Pascal by initialising a procedure variable with the specific procedure satisfying the actual specification of the component. Passing this procedure variable as a parameter allows to easily fill the component in such a way that the shell-like structure is finally fully in conformance with the specific needs of the given application environment. This is evidently a smart way of fostering total re-use in situations where lack of parameterisation would otherwise require modification of the components.

The effectiveness of the approach is enhanced if the language supports the concept of data types that are members of *one* family. This concept is known in various languages under names like: inheritance, type extension, class prefixing, and even type casting can be used to support this purpose.

It should be noted that parameterisation by procedural parameters not only leaves room for flexibility when such a parameterised procedure gets instantiated, this flexibility implies also that the semantics of such a component are incomplete in a sense. Since software normalisation as proposed by Mittermeir builds on semantic criteria, they cannot (as of current) be applied to skeletal procedures before they are instantiated with their actual procedure parameters.

This, as well as efficiency considerations, gave rise to lengthy discussions at the workshop. However, one might say that these are not severe obstacles in either direction. As has been shown by Goguen, parameterisation, if coached and controlled by appropriate mechanisms, is a concept which can be easily understood. Since the relational specifications, on which normalisation builds, does allow for non-determinism, it can account for parameterisation. It could even be extended in such a way as to answer the question of what constitutes legitimate parameter sets, such being also a yardstick for "good taste" in this respect. (However, it has to be mentioned that this still needs to be formalised.)

Another question which came up, is whether we need formal yardsticks for things which good designers will do and have done since ages anyway. We might not, if, we work in a small group environment on well understood problems. However, if we are heading towards application and system building on large problems and on the technological frontier respectively, the unaided eye of even the best software engineer — and by definition not all software engineers are the best — will not be sufficient to identify all small spots of impurity, which after integration may bring a system towards the brink of collapse.

2.4 REVERSE ENGINEERING

Abstract of the discussion on domain analysis during the reuse workshop, SERC, Utrecht, the Netherlands, 23-24 November 1989
Participants to the discussion: P. Hall (reporter), J. van Katwijk, K. Lano, W. Rossak, J. Zhang

The major objective of Software Reverse Engineering is to develop or extract higher level descriptions of a software system from its lower level source code description (Rich 1988, Sneed 1989, and the recent special issue of IEEE Software of January 1990). The higher level description of source code may be

- the collection of comments from well documented source code units such as procedures and functions in Pascal,

- a collection of recursively defined procedures or first-order predicates in some very high level languages such as Lisp and Prolog,

- a partition into high level modules of the source code (Parnas 1972).

- data-flow diagrams, entity grid charts and structure charts, entity life history matrices, logical dialogue outlines for dialogue design, and other products of structured analysis (Martin 1985 and Pressman 1987).

- an object-oriented description of the software

- a formal specification in a notation like Z (Spivey 1988)

The intention of the above reverse engineering is to be able to understand the code, but for software re-use we want to do more — we want to identify coherent bodies of code which can be made available for re-use, possibly after suitable generalisation and improvement.

Supposing we were able to use clues in the code to segment it into potentially useful components, we would still need to describe the software and generate some higher level description of it, and even naming the putative component (unless it has been named in the code) may be problematic. Arbitrary naming will render any higher level specification useless simply because it will provide no clue to the component's function, so we need a meaningful name. The important role that names and identifiers play in understanding source code has been well argued by Biggerstaff 1989.

To be able to name a component, we need to know what the possible names are — we do need to understand the application domain in which the software was intended to operate. To do this we need to undertake a **domain analysis**.

This domain analysis would identify the useful components and their interrelationships. The components would exist in a hierarchy or lattice, and would be associated with composition rules to indicate which combinations of components are meaningful. In analysing code or text, the constraints imposed by the composition rules would help resolve ambiguities. The ultimate manifestation of this domain knowledge would be as a domain specific language which could be, if suitably formal, an application specific programming language.

In making the abstraction and analysis, we will in general have to address not just one domain, but a hierarchy of domains, perhaps even a calculus of these. We may well abstract from the level of program code, where the domain is that of programming, through several technical design domains, through to a generic application domain involving concepts like database management systems and order-processing systems, before reaching a particular application domain. We may have broader and narrower domains, and be able to combine domains and regard domains as equivalent. In order to obtain adequate re-use we may need to consider describing a component within a broader domain, while in order to get useful descriptions we may need to seek a narrower domain.

Thus the process of reverse engineering will involve a process of identifying possible components taking regard to the domain under consideration, evaluating whether this is a good component, and then repeating this across the software at a particular level and up the levels of hierarchy, as is shown in the figure 2.3.

The individual steps are elaborated on below:

identify components syntactic structures such as procedure begin and end, loops, etc, may demarcate a potential component, and information flow analysis may also help, to show where the clean interfaces are.

Metrics for good modularisation such as cohesion and coupling from the design domain, may further help.

Even application domain knowledge may help identify objects, and rules of composition may eliminate some choices once adjacent components have been

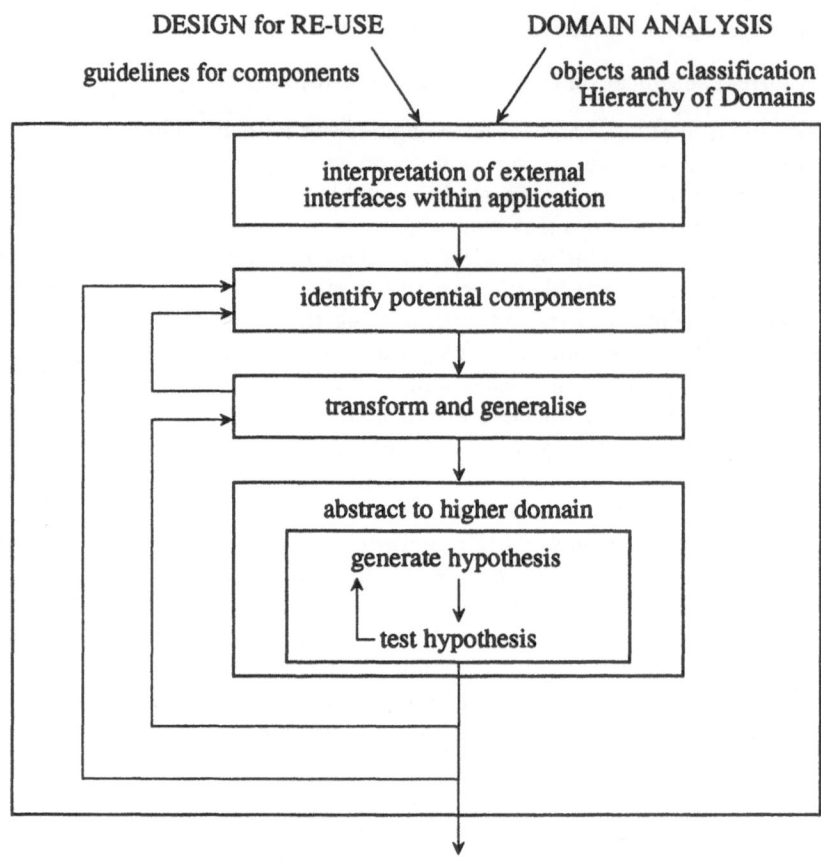

Figure 2.3 Reverse Engineering Process

identified.

The lowest level domain may be eliminated first completely, in translation to intermediate language — an approach taken by both the REDO project, and static analysis tools like MALPAS and SPADE (Carre 89). It may be appropriate to standardise this language, though it can be argued that it is premature to do so.

Transform and Generalise. Changes are made within a single domain, restructuring and paraphrasing the description. At the code level this could lead to the discovery of iterations, the conversion to or elimination of recursion, or changes to data structures. Transformations used would have been proven to preserve correctness.

abstraction — movement to a higher level domain .

Hypothesis generation — match patterns and templates, look at comments and variable names, consult the user, consult the environment to look at the uses.

hypothesis testing — verification or proof, execution of the code on key test cases, check position in environment

With highly formalised programming languages, the code itself may reveal much information, but abstraction above the level of the code cannot proceed without knowledge from higher level domains. This domain knowledge must be available, and some process of associating the higher level domain with the lower level description in code or design descriptions must be available. It is here that the comments and documentation are seen as vitally important.

2.5 DEVELOPMENT WITH RE-USE

Abstract of the discussion on domain analysis during the reuse workshop, SERC, Utrecht, the Netherlands, 23-24 November 1989
Participants to the discussion: C. Boldyreff, R. Adams, J. Cramer, Th. de Ridder, E. Dijkstra, N. Haddley, N. Maiden and B. Sijtsma

In order to be able to Develop or Design Software using Re-usable components, we need to provide methods and support for the following:

- a software development lifecycle incorporating re-use

- strategies for adaptation and interconnection of re-usable components

- support for checking the correct use of interfaces and for the coherence of composite systems

- re-use decision support allowing costs and benefits of re-use to be estimated

- information service resource centre about the re-usable software components

- versioning and development histories — software component log books

- means of capturing development histories so strategies to development can be re-used

- means of exploring new relations between existing components

There is a useful distinction to be made between "Industrial Re-use" and "Research Re-use". These are long term re-use and short term re-use respectively, and there is a real difference between them. However, even if we equate industrial re-use with black box re-use and research/exploratory programming re-use with white box re-use, there is clearly a need for "Gray Box re-use", where we allow changes to re-usable software components, but formally control them.

It is not clear that different development models/methods are needed to incorporate re-use. There is a good natural fit between re-use and a transformational approach to software development, between re-use and formal approaches where items from algebraic specification language or Z libraries are re-used. However, it can be problematic if the developer wishes to combine into a single system specification items written in Z, VDM and OBJ; and more generally, there is the possibility of world or underlying model collision when pre-specified items are combined. However, standard decomposition into subtasks is difficult. Re-use possibilities need to be known upstream in the development process; perhaps, even by the customer in order to influence the requirements. There is a need for improved mechanisms for communication of results, facilitating subsequent re-use.

In cataloguing re-usable software, there is a trade-off between the effort needed to describe components adequately and the effort to actually re-use the components. Little effort is required to describe software informally using keywords; but the informality of the descriptions means re-use is harder. To formally describe re-usable software requires a considerable effort; and such formality may be unnecessary. Tools supporting informal descriptions such as structured design notations may be the happy medium. In the trade-off between formality and informality, tools to support **exploration** are needed.

For example, such tools might include component understanding tools (eg. HP Microscope), Computer Assisted Learning (intelligent tool tutors), etc.

It is not clear whether further research and development is needed in the area of interconnection languages. On the one hand, renaming etc. are straight forward and there is no real research needed here. On the other hand, it is not clear how the interconnection of components described in mixed notations is best effected. Can we avoid translating to a common base language?

Tools are needed to support redesign of existing systems where the motivation is to **clean-up** an operational system by introducing more reliable proven components. The German word **sanierung** was suggested as an appropriate descriptor for this activity.

Following the above discussion, we see that some very firm requirements arise on the other parts of the software re-use environment.

From Component Engineering (Reverse Engineering and Design for Re-use) we require:

- Guidelines for Re-usable Component Design, so newly designed software is really re-usable

- Robust and Correct Components, with documented measures of these properties

- Fully explained Components, where the purpose, development history, and other information is available

- Black and White Box Components, where the code cannot be changed, and where it can be changed.

- Support for **sanierung**

From Domain Analysis we require:

- Languages — text book like information in addition to a standard language (ie. domain vocabulary to describe its software). DRACO-like languages are of little utility to us.

- Taxonomies of components and Road Maps showing relationships between concepts and components

- Standards — for quality. These are needed in finding components, choosing amongst components, understanding them, and for naming them.

- Focus, not breadth. There is trade-off between narrow domains resulting in good but limited re-use, and wide domains resulting in poor but potentially widespread re-use.

- Analogy — We need to be able to move across domains making use of analogical reasoning, perhaps with known mappings between domains being given formally.

Finally we need to be able to feedback suggestions for potentially re-usable components to Design for Re-use (and indeed to Reverse Engineering).

Chapter 3

Reuse Bibliography

With thanks to the Ada-Europe Reuse Workgroup.

Adelson B, Soloway E. The Role of Domain Experience in Software Design. IEEE Transactions on Software Engineering 1985 11; 11:1351-60

Afshar SK. Software Reuse Via Source Transformation. In: Proceedings of COMP-SAC 85. IEEE Computer Society Press, Washington, DC, USA, Oct 1985, pp 54-61

Albrechtson H. Software Concepts: Knowledge Organisation and the human interface. In: Fugmann R. (ed) Tools for Knowledge Organization and the Human Interface; Advances in Knowledge Organisation, Proceedings of ISKO conference, Dortmund, August 1990, vol 1 & 2. Indeks, Frankfurt am Main, 1990 pp 48-63

Alexandridis NA. Adaptable Software and Hardware: Problems and Solutions. Computer 1986 19; 2:29-39

Allen RC. SOFTBUS — An Approach to Software Engineering for Distributed Real-Time Long-Lifetime Spacecraft Data Management Systems. In: Nickols HK, Simpson D. (eds) ESEC'87; 1st European Software Engineering Conference, Strassbourg, France, Sept 1987. Springer, Berlin, pp 217-226 (Lecture Notes in Computer Science 289)

Ambras JP, Berlin LM, Chiarelli ML, Foster AL, O'Day V, Splitter RN. MicroScope: An Integrated Program Analysis Tool. Hewlett-Packard Journal, August 1988;

Anderson JA. Exploiting Generics in Ada Training. In: Wallis PJL. (ed) Ada: Managing the Transition. Proceedings of the Ada-Europe International Conference Edinburgh 6-8 May 1986. Cambridge University Press, 1986, pp 217-226 (Ada Companion Series)

Antonini P. et al. Maintenance and Reverse Engineering: Low-level Design Documents Production and Improvement. In: Martin RJ. (chair) Proceedings of the Conference on Software Maintenance; Austin, Texas, September 21-24, 1987, IEEE Computer Society Press, Washington DC, 1987 pp 91-100

Aoyama M, Suzuki T, Suzuki M, Fujimoto H. Development of Telecommunications Software Based on Paradigms. In: Proceedings Software Engineering for Telecommunication Switching Systems, 6th International Conference, 1986. IEE, London, England 1986 pp 112-117

Arango G. et al. Maintenance and Porting of Software by Design Recovery. In:

Proceedings Conference on Software Maintenance. IEEE Computer Society Press, Los Alamitos, California, 1985, pp 42-49

Arango G, Freeman P. Modelling Knowledge for Software Development. In: International Workshop on Software Specification and Design. IEEE Computer Society Press, 1985, pp 63-66

Arango G. Domain Analysis: From Art to Engineering Discipline. Proceedings Fifth International Workshop on Software Specification and Design; Pittsburgh, Pennsylvannia, USA, May 19-20, 1989. Software Engineering Notes 1989 14; 3:152-159

Arango G. Evaluation of a Reuse-based Software Construction Technology. Department of Information and Computer Science, University of California

Arango G. Domain Engineering for Mechanical Reuse. Department of Information and Computer Science, University of California

Arkwright TD. Global Issues in Reuse from a real project. In: Wallis PJL. (ed) Ada: Managing the Transition. Proceedings of the Ada-Europe International Conference Edinburgh 6-8 May 1986. Cambridge University Press, 1986, pp 13-22 (Ada Companion Series)

Arnold RS. (ed) Tutorial on Software Restructuring. IEEE Computer Society Press, 1986

Arthur JD. An Interactive Environment for Tool Selection, Specification, and Composition. Technical Report TR-86-2, Department of Computing, Virginia Polytechnic Institute, Blackburg, VA, USA, 1986

Ausnit C, Braun C, Sterling E, Goodenough J, Simpson R. Ada Reusability Guidelines. Report no 3285-2-208/2, SofTech Inc., Waltham, MA, April 1985

Ayers GA, Curry RM. Experience with Traits in the Xerox Star Workstation. IEEE Transactions on Software Engineering Sept 1984 10; 5:519-527

Balzer R, Goldman N, Wile D. Informality in Program Specifications. IEEE Transactions on Software Engineering, March 1978 4; 2:94-103

Balzer R. Evolution as a New Basis for Reusability. In: Proceedings of COMPSAC 84. IEEE Computer Society Press. Silver Spring, MD, USA, Nov 1984, pp 471-473

Barnard JH, Mertz RF, Price AL. A Recommended Practice for Describing Software Designs: IEEE Standards Project 1016. IEEE Transactions on Software Engineering 1986 12; 2:258-263

Barra S, Ghisio S, Gouthier O, Truzzi P. An Environment Providing Assistance in Code Reusability. In: Proceedings Software Engineering for Telecommunication Switching Systems, 6th International Conference, 1986. IEE, London, England pp 221-225

Barra S, Ghisio S, Gouthier O, Truzzi P. Assisted Reusability of CHILL Programs. CSELT Tech. Rep. Italy, April 1986 14; 2:111-115

Barstow D. Knowledge-Based Program Construction. Elsevier North-Holland, 1979

Barstow DR. A Perspective on Automatic Programming. AI Magazine, 1984; Spring 5-27

Barstow DR. Domain-Specific Automatic Programming. IEEE Transactions on Software Engineering Nov 1985 11; 11:1321-1336

Bassett PG. Frame-Based Software Engineering. IEEE Software, July 1987 4; 4:9-16

Berard EV. Software Reusability Cannot Be Considered in a Vacuum. In: Michael GA. (chair) Intellectual Leverage; Spring COMPCON 87; 32nd International Conference, San Francisco, Feb 1987, Digest of Papers. IEEE Computer Society Press Washington DC, Spring 1987, pp 390-393

Biggerstaff T. A Radical Hypothesis: Reusability is the Essence of Design. In: Proceedings of COMPSAC 84. IEEE Computer Society Press, Silver Spring, MD, USA, Nov 1984, pp 474-475

Biggerstaff TJ, Perlis AJ. Foreword on Reusability. IEEE Transactions on Software Engineering Sept 1984 10; 5:474-476

Biggerstaff TJ. Software Technology Program. MCC Technical Report No STP-202-87. Microelectronics and Computer Technology Corporation (MCC) 1987

Biggerstaff T, Richter C. Reusability Framework, Assessment, and Directions. IEEE Software 1987 4; 2:41-49

Biggerstaff TJ. Design Recovery for Maintenance and Reuse. IEEE Computer, July 1989 22; 7:36-49

Biggerstaff TJ, Perlis AJ. Software Reusability, vol 1& 2. ACM Press 1989 (Frontier Series)

Boldyreff C. Automating the Analysis of Source Code to Support Reuse: A Survey of Relevant Work and Available Tools. Paper submitted to Toulouse '89 Second International Workshop: Software Engineering and its Applications.

Boldyreff C. Reuse, Software Concepts, Descriptive Methods and the Practitioner Project. ACM SIGSOFT Software Engineering Notes, 1989 14; 2:25-31

Boldyreff C, Hall P. Reusability: Evaluation of Practitioner Project Experience and Future Directions. In: CASE 89 Advance Working Papers. Imperial College London July 1989 pp 470-471

Boldyreff C, Zhang J. From Recursion Abstraction to Automated Commenting — A Transformational Approach towards Reverse Engineering of Software to Support Reusability. PRACTITIONER, Working Paper, Department of Computer Science, Brunel University, December 1989

Boldyreff C, Elzer P, Hall P, Kaaber U, Keilmann J, Witt J. PRACTITIONER: Pragmatic Support for the Reuse of Concepts in Existing Software. Submitted to

SE90

Booch G. Software Components With Ada, Benjamin/Cummings, Menlo Park, California, 1987

Bott MF, Elliot A, Gautier RJ. Ada Reuse Guidelines. ECLIPSE/REUSE/DST/-ADA-GUIDE/RP, Software Sciences Ltd. 1986

Bott MF. Software Reuse — An Overview. In: IEE Colloquium on Reusable Software Components (Digest No. 68). IEE, London, England, 1987, pp 28

Bowles K. Software Components Industry. In: Ada-Europe/Ada TEC Joint Conference. March 1983, Comm. Eur. Communities, Brussels, Belgium, 1983

Boyle JM, Muralidharan MN. Program Reusability Through Program Transformation. IEEE Transactions on Software Engineering Sept 1984 10; 5:574-588

Braun CL, Goodenough JB, Eanes RS. Ada Reusability Guidelines. TR 3285-2-208/2, SoftTech Inc., April 1985

Brena. Program Synthesis through Problem Splitting. Computers & AI Czech, 1985 4; 5:421-9

Brodie ML, Mylopoulos J, Schmidt JW. (eds) On Conceptual Modelling: Perspectives from Artificial Intelligence, Databases, and Programming Languages. Springer-Verlag, New York 1984 (Topics in Information Systems)

Bron C. On Reusable Software. In: Proceedings Ada-Europe/Ada TEC Joint Conference. March 1983, Comm. Eur. Communities, Brussels, Belgium, 1983

Bruns GR, Gerhart SL, Johnson C, Yaung A. Design Technology Assessments: Affirm, CAEDE, Draco and PNUT. MCC Technical Report No STP-179-87, Microelectronics and Computer Technology Corporation (MCC), June 1987

Burton BA, Broido MD. A Phased Approach to Ada Package Reuse. In: Proceedings of Software Technology for Adaptable Reliable Systems (STARS) Workshop. April 1985, pp 83-98

Burton BA, Broido MD. Development of an Ada Package Library. In: Proceedings 1st Conference on Ada Programming Applications for the NASA Space Station. Houston, June 1986

Burton BA, Aragon RW, Bailey SA, Koehler KD, Mayes LA. The Reusable Software Library. IEEE Software 1987 4; 4:25-33

Carbonell JG. Derivational Analogy: A Theory of Reconstructive Problem Solving and Expertise Acquisition. Technical Report CMU-CS-85-115. Computer Science Department, Carnegie-Mellon University, Pittsburgh, March 1985

Carstensen HB. A Real Example of Reusing Ada Software. In: Proceedings of the Second National Conference on Software Reusability and Maintainability. National Institute for Software Quality and Productivity, Washington, DC, March 1987 pp

B1-B19

Cavaliere MJ, Archambleault PJ. Reusable Code at the Hartford Insurance Company. In: Proceedings of the Workshop on Reusability in Programming. ITT, Shelton, Conn, USA, 1983, pp 273-278

Cheatham TE.Jr. Reusability Through Program Transformations. IEEE Transactions on Software Engineering 1984 10; 5:589-594

Chikofsky EJ, Cross JHII. Reverse Engineering and Design Recovery: a Taxonomy. IEEE Software January 1990; 1:13-18

Clapp J. Software Reusability: A Management View. In: Proceedings of COMP-SAC 84. IEEE Computer Society Press, Silver Spring, MD, USA, Nov 1984, pp 479-480

Coelho EMP. Cognitive Issues in Software Reuse. AD-A159386/2 Naval Postgraduate School, June 1985

Conn R. The Ada Software Repository. In: Michael GA. (chair) Intellectual Leverage; Spring COMPCON 87; 32nd International Conference, San Francisco, Feb 1987, Digest of Papers. IEEE Computer Society Press Washington DC, Spring 1987, pp 372-275

Conradi R. Knowledge Based Assistants for Programming Environments (unpublished draft document). Norwegian Institute for Technology, Trondheim, Norway, 1987

Cross A. Design Intelligence: The Use of Codes and Language Systems. Design Studies 1986 7; 1:14-19

Curry GA, Ayers RM. Experience with Traits in the Xerox Star Workstation. IEEE Transactions on Software Engineering 1984 10; 5:519-527

Dausmann M. The Application of Multiple Libraries to Reuse Existing Software in Ada. Doc. Ref. Ada Reuse MD87/3, I.I. Biometric Institute, 1987

St.-Dennis R, Stachour P, Frankowski E, Onuegbe E. Measurable Characteristics of Reusable Ada Software. Ada Letters March/April 1986 6; 2:41-50

Deutsch LP. Reusablily in the Smalltalk-80 Programming System. In: Proceedings of the ITT Workshop on Reusability in Programming; Stratford, Connecticut, ITT, Newport, RI, Sept 7-9, 1983. pp 72-76

Dhama HS, Shtern V. A Net Method for Specification of Reusable Software. Proceedings Fifth International Workshop on Software Specification and Design; Pittsburgh, Pennsylvannia, USA, May 19-20, 1989. Software Engineering Notes 1989 14; 3:137-139

Dillistone BR. Configuration Management within an IPSE and its Implications for Software Re-Use. In: Brereton P. (ed) Software Engineering Environments. Horwood Chichester England, 1988 (Ellis Horwood Books on Information Technology)

Dusink EM, van Katwijk J. Reflections on Reusable Software and Software Components. In: Tafvelin S. (ed) Ada Components: Libraries and Tools. Proceedings of the Ada-Europe International Conference, Stockholm 26-28 May 1987. Cambridge University Press, U.K., 1987, pp 113-126 (Ada Companion Series)

Embley DW, Woodfield SN. A Knowledge Structure for Reusing Abstract Data Types. In: Ada Software Production; Proceedings of the Joint Ada Conference, Fifth National Conference on Ada Technology and Washington Ada Symposium. U.S. Army Communications-Electronics Command, Fort Monmouth, New Jersey, 1987, pp 27-34

Embley DW, Woodfield SN. A Knowledge Structure for Reusing Abstract Data Types. In: Proceedings of the 9th International Conference on Software Engineering, March 30 - April 2 1987, Monterey, California, USA. IEEE Computer Society Press, Washington, DC, USA, 1987, pp 360-368

Feather M. Reuse in the Context of a Transformation Based Methodology. In: Proceedings of the ITT Workshop on Reusability in Programming, Stratford, Connecticut, ITT, Newport, RI, September 7-9, 1983

Fischer G. Cognitive View of Reuse and Redesign. IEEE Software, 1987 4; 4:60-72

Fischer G, Lemke AC, Rathke C. From design to redesign. In: Proceedings of the 9th International Conference on Software Engineering, March 30 - April 2 1987, Monterey, California, USA. IEEE Computer Society Press, Washington, DC, USA, 1987

Fischer G, Lemke AC. Construction Kits and Design Environments: Steps Toward Human Problem Domain Communication. Department of Computer Science and Institute of Cognative Science, University of Colorado, 1988

Foster JR, Munro M. A Documentation Method Based on Cross-referencing. In: Martin RJ. (chair) Proceedings of the Conference on Software Maintenance; Austin, Texas, September 21-24, 1987, IEEE Computer Society Press, Washington DC, 1987 pp 181-185

Frakes BA. Nejmeh WB. Software Reuse Through Information Retrieval. In: Proceedings of the 20th Hawaii International Conference on System Sciences. Hawaii Int. Conference Syst. Sci., Honolulu, HI, USA, 1987, Western Periodicals Company, Honolulu, HI, USA. pp 530-535

Frankowski EN. Why Programs Built from Reusable Software Should be Single Paradigm. In: Proceedings of the STARS Reusability Workshop, March 24-27, 1986, pp 24-27

Freeman P. Reusable Software Engineering: Concept and Research Direction. In: Proceedings of the ITT Workshop on Reusability in Programming, Stratford, Connecticut, ITT, Newport, RI, September 7-9, 1983

Freeman P. A Conceptual Analysis of the Draco Approach to Constructing Software Systems. In: Freeman P. (ed) Tutorial: Software Reusability. IEEE Computer Society Press, Washington, DC, 1987

Freeman P. (ed) Tutorial: Software Reusability. IEEE Computer Society Press, Washington, DC, 1987

Gargaro A, Pappas T. Understanding Ada Software Reusability Issues for the Transition of Mission Critical Computer Resource Applications. In: Wallis PJL. (ed) Ada: Managing the Transition. Proceedings of the Ada-Europe International Conference Edinburgh 6-8 May 1986. Cambridge University Press, 1986, pp 105-114 (Ada Companion Series)

Gautier RJ. A Language for Describing Ada Software Components. In: Tafvelin S. (ed) Ada Components: Libraries and Tools. Proceedings of the Ada-Europe International Conference, Stockholm 26-28 May 1987. Cambridge University Press, U.K., 1987, pp 75-85 (Ada Companion Series)

Gargaro A, Pappas TL. Reusability Issues and Ada. IEEE Software 1987 4; 4:43-51

Geary K. Practical Problems in Introducing Software Reuse. In: IEE Colloquium on 'Reusable Software Components' (Digest No. 68). IEE, London, England, 1987

Genillard C, Ebel N. Reusability of Software Components in the Building of Syntax-Driven Software Tools Written in Ada. In: Wallis PJL. (ed) Ada: Managing the Transition. Proceedings of the Ada-Europe International Conference Edinburgh 6-8 May 1986. Cambridge University Press, 1986, pp 125-135 (Ada Companion Series)

Gerhart S. Reusability lessons from verification technology. In: Proceedings of the ITT Workshop on Reusability in Programming, Stratford, Connecticut. ITT, Newport, RI, Sept 7-9, 1983

Goguen JA. Parameterized Programming. IEEE Transactions on Software Engineering Sept 1984 10; 5:528-543

Goguen JA. Reusing and Interconnecting Software Components. IEEE Computer 1986 19; 2:16-28

Grover V, Guerrieri E. Expressing Module Interconnections in Ada. In: Wallis PJL. (ed) Ada: Managing the Transition. Proceedings of the Ada-Europe International Conference Edinburgh 6-8 May 1986. Cambridge University Press, 1986, pp 273-280 (Ada Companion Series)

Hall PAV. Reusable and Reconfigurable Software Using C. In: Brown P. (ed) Proceedings of Software Engineering-86. IEE Computing Series 6, Peter Peregrinus Ltd., U.K., 1986 Chapter 12

Hall PAV. Software Components and Reuse. Computer Bulletin of the BCS Dec 1987; 14-20

Hall PAV. Software Components and Reuse — Getting More out of Your Code. Information & Software Technology U.K. Jan/Feb 1987 29; 1:

Hall P, Boldyreff C. Software Reuse. In: McDermid J. (ed) Software Engineering

Reference Book. Butterworths, U.K., forthcoming,

Hansen GA, Spoulding SD, Edgar G. Certification of Ada Parts for Reuse. In: Proceedings 1st Conference on Ada Programming Applications for the NASA Space Slation. Houston, June 1986

Harandi MT, Ning JQ. Knowledge-Based Program Analysis. IEEE Software January 1990; 1:74-81

Henderson P, Warboys B. An Architectural Framework for Systems. ICL Journal May 1989;

Hill J. Reusable Code. Unisphere USA, Aug 1985 5; 5:22-24

Horowitz JB, Munson E. An Expansive View of Reusable Software. IEEE Transactions on Software Engineering Sept 1984 10; 5:477-487

Horowitz E. Fundamentals of Programming Languages. Springer- Verlag, 1987

Hulkkonen TO, Keha NM. Software Component Library. In: Wallis PJL. (ed) Ada: Managing the Transition. Proceedings of the Ada-Europe International Conference Edinburgh 6-8 May 1986. Cambridge University Press, 1986, pp 175-182 (Ada Companion Series)

ISO 2788-1986, Documentation - Guidelines for establishment and development of monolingual thesauri

ISO 5964-1985; Documentation - Guidelines for establishment and development of multilingual thesauri

Isoda S. Quality Assurance and Software Reuse Activities with Multi-Firm Joint Teams. In: Proceedings 10th Anniversary COMPSAC'86. IEEE Computer Society Press, Washington, DC, USA, October 1986

Jandrasics G. SOFTDOC: A System for Automated Software Analysis and Documentation. In: Proceedings of ACM Workshop on Software Quality Assurance April, 1981

Johnson WC. Reusable Software. Masters Thesis AD-A146575/6, Naval Postgraduate School, March 1984

Johnson WL. Overview of the Knowledge-Based Specification Assistant. USC/Information Sciences Institute. Marina del Rey, CA 90292,

Johnson WL, Soloway E. Proust: Knowledge-Based Program Understanding. IEEE Transactions on Software Engineering Nov 1985 11; 3:267-275,

Jones G. Software Reusability: Approaches and Issues. In: Proceedings of COMPSAC'84. IEEE Computer Society Press, Silver Spring, NM, USA, Nov 1984, pp 476-478

Jones H, Krasner B, Litvintchouk H, Mellby J, Mungle J, Willman H. Issues in Software Reusability. ACM Ada Letters March-April 1985 4; 5:97-99

Jones H, Krasner B, Litvinchouk H, Mellby S, Mungle J, Willman J. Issues in Software Reusability. SIGSOFT Software Engineering Notes, April 1985 10; 2:108-109

Jones TC. (ed) Tutorial: Programmer Productivity: Issues for the Eighties. IEEE Computer Society Press, 1983

Jones TC. Reusability in Programming: A Survey of the State of the Art. IEEE Transactions on Software Engineering 1984 10; 5:487-493

Jones TC. (ed) Tutorial: Programming Productivity: Issues for The Eighties. Second Edition, IEEE Computer Society Press, Washington, DC, 1986

Kaiser GE, Garlan D. Melding Software Systems from Reusable Building Blocks. IEEE Software 1987 4; 4:17-24

Kandt K. Pegasus: A Tool for the Acquisition and Reuse of Software Designs. In: Proceedings of COMPSAC 84. IEEE Computer Society Press, Silver Spring, MD, USA, Nov 1984, pp 288-293

Kant E, Barstow D. The Refinement Paradigm: The Interaction of Coding and Efficiency Knowledge in Program Synthesis. IEEE Transactions on Software Engineering Sept 1981 7; 5:458-471

Karakostas V. Requirements for CASE Tools in Early Software Reuse. Software Engineering Notes April 1989 14; 2:39-41

Karimi J, Konsyski BR. An Automated Design Assistant. IEEE Transactions on Software Engineering Febr 1988 14; 2:194-210

Kass R, Finn T. Rules for Implicit Acquisition of Knowledge about the User. University of Pennsylvania, Computing and Information Science, Philadelphia, PA 19104, USA

Katz S, Richter CA, The K-S. PARIS: A System for Reusing Partially Interpreted Schemas. In: Proceedings of the 9th International Conference on Software Engineering. IEEE Computer Society Press, Washington, DC, USA, 1987, pp 377-389

Kazaczynski W, Ning JQ. SRE: A Knowledge-based Environment for Large-Scale Software Re-engineering Activities. In: Proceedings of the International Conference on Software Engineering. IEEE Computer Society Press, 1989

Keenan P. The Reuse of Design as a First Step towards the Introduction of Ada Components. Ada User 1987 8 (Supplement); 33-41

Kernighan BW. The UNIX System and Software Reusability. IEEE Transactions on Software Engineering Sept 1984 10; 5:513-518

Krampell CS, Collberg MG. A Property-Based Method for Selecting Among Multiple Implementations of Modules. In: Nickols HK, Simpson D. (eds) ESEC'87; 1st European Software Engineering Conference, Strassbourg, France, Sept 1987. Springer, Berlin, pp 207-216 (Lecture Notes in Computer Science 289)

Lanergan RG, Dugan DK. Software Engineering with Reusable Design and Code. In: Mills H. (chair) Productivity; an Urgent Priority; Proceedings 23rd IEEE Computer Society International Conference, COMPCON Fall 81 Washington, DC, Sept 1981, pp 296-303

Lanergan RG, Grasso CA. Reusable Designs and Code: a Strategy for Designing Software with Maintenance in Mind. In: Arnold RS (ed) Software Maintenance; Workshop Record, Dec 1983, Monterey, CA. IEEE Computer Society Press, 1984, pp 55-56

Lanergan RG, Grasso CA. Software Engineering with Reusable Designs and Code. IEEE Transactions on Software Engineering Sept 1984 10; 5:498-501

Ledbetter L, Cox B. Software-ICs: A Plan for Building Reusable Software Components. BYTE June 1985; 307-316

Lenz M, Schmid HA, Wolf PF. Software Reuse through Building Blocks. IEEE Software 1987 4; 4:34-42

Levy P, Ripken K. Experience in Constructing Ada Programs from Non-Trivial Reusable Modules. In: Tafvelin S. (ed) Ada Components: Libraries and Tools. Proceedings of the Ada-Europe International Conference, Stockholm 26-28 May 1987. Cambridge University Press, U.K., 1987, pp 100-112 (Ada Companion Series)

Lewis TG, Eissa IF. A Programmer's Database for Reusable Modules. In: Proceedings 4th Annual Pacific Northwest Software Quality Conference on Software Excellence, 1986. pp 273-292

Litke D. A Design for a Reusable Ada Library. In: Proceedings 1st Conference on Ada Programming Applications for the NASA Space Station, Houston, June 1986

Litvintchouk SD, Matsumoto AS. Design of Ada Systems Yielding Reusable Components: An Approach Using Structured Algebraic Specification. IEEE Transactions on Software Engineering Sept 1984 10; 5:544-551

London RL, Milsted KR. Specifying and Verifying Reusable Components Using Z: Sets and Dictionaries. Proceedings Fifth International Workshop on Software Specification and Design; Pittsburgh, Pennsylvannia, USA, May 19-20, 1989. Software Engineering Notes 1989 14; 3:120-127

Lubars MD. Affording Higher Reliability Through Software Reusability. SIGSOFT Software Engineering Notes Oct 1986 11; 5:39-42

Lubars MD. Code Reusability in the Large versus Code Reusability in the Small. SIGSOFT Software Engineering Notes Jan 1986 11; 1:21-28

Lubars MD. Wide-Spectrum Support for Software Reusability. Technical Report STP-276-87. MCC, August 1987

Lubars MD, Harandi MT. Knowledge-Based Software Design Using Design Schemas. In: Proceedings of the 9th International Conference on Software Engineering, 30th March - 2nd April 1987. IEEE Computer Society Press, Washington, DC, USA,

1987, pp 253-262

MacAnAirchinnigh C. Reusable Generic Packages: Design Guidelines Based on Structural Isomorphism. In: Proceedings 3rd Annual National Conference on Ada Technology; Hyatt Regency Houston, Houston, Texas, March 1985. US Army Communications-Electronics Command Fort Monmouth, NJ, US Army, Center for Tactical Computer Systems, 1985, pp 132-144

MacAnAirchinnigh M. Conceptual Model of an Ada Software Factory. Ada-Europe Environment Working Group. Internal report, 1987

MacAnAirchinnigh C, Burns M, Chedgey A. Reusable Units — Construction Methods and Measure. In: Tafvelin S. (ed) Ada Components: Libraries and Tools. Proceedings of the Ada-Europe International Conference, Stockholm 26-28 May 1987. Cambridge University Press, U.K., 1987, pp 127-140 (Ada Companion Series)

Machida S. Approaches to Software Reusability in Telecommunications Software Systems. In: Proceedings of COMPSAC 85 IEEE Computer Society Press, Washington, DC, USA, Oct 1985

Margono J, Berard EV. A Modified Booch's Taxonomy for Ada Generic Data Structure Components and Thier Implementation. In: Tafvelin S. (ed) Ada Components: Libraries and Tools. Proceedings of the Ada-Europe International Conference, Stockholm 26-28 May 1987. Cambridge University Press, U.K., 1987, pp 61-74 (Ada Companion Series)

Martin J, McClure C. Diagramming Techniques for Analysts and Programmers. Prentice-Hall 1985

Masters MW, Kuchinski MJ. Software Design Prototyping Using Ada. Ada Letters Jan-Febr 1983 2; 4:68-75

Matsumoto SD, Litvintchouk AS. Design of Ada Systems Yielding Reusable Components: An Approach Using Structured Algebraic Specification. IEEE Transactions on Software Engineering Sept 1984 10; 5:544-551

Matsumoto Y. Organizational Effort for Reusing Existing Softwares. In: Proceedings of COMPCON Fall '84. IEEE Computer Society Press. Silver Spring, VA, USA, Sept 1984

Matsumoto Y. Some Experience in Promoting Reusable Software: Presentation in Higher Abstract Levels. IEEE Transactions on Software Engineering Sept 1984 10; 5:502-512

McCain R. A Software Development Methodology for Reusable Components. In: Proceedings of the Eighteenth Hawaii International Conference on System Sciences. Western Periodicals Company, Honolulu, HI, USA, Jan 1985, pp 319-324

McIllroy MD. Mass-Produced Software Components. In: Buxton JM, Naur P, Randell B. Software Engineering Concepts and Techniques; 1968 NATO Conference on Software Engineering. Petrocelli/Charter, Belgium , 1976, pp 88-98

32

McWilliams G. Users See a CASE Advance in Reverse Engineering Tools. Datamation Febr 1, 1988; 30-36

Mendal GO. Micro Issues in Reuse from a Real Project. Ada Technology Support Laboratory. Lockheed Missiles and Space Company Inc., Sunnyvale, CA, 1985

Mendal GO. Designing for Ada Reuse: A Case Study. In: IEEE Computer Society Second International Conference on Ada Applications and Environments, April 8-10 1986, Miami Beach, FL. IEEE Los Angelos 1986 pp 33-42

Metcalf SG. Software Library. A Reusable Software Issue (AD-AI50722/7). Naval Postgraduate School, June 1984

Meyer B. Eiffel: Programming for Reusability and Extendibility. SIGPLAN Notices Febr 1987 22; 2:85-94

Meyer B. Reusability: The Case for Object-Oriented Design. IEEE Software March 1987 4; 2:50-64

Meyer B, Nerson M, Matsuo JM. EIFFEL: Object-Oriented Design for Software Engineering. In: Nickols HK, Simpson D. (eds) ESEC'87; 1st European Software Engineering Conference, Strassbourg, France, Sept 1987. Springer, Berlin, pp 237-245 (Lecture Notes in Computer Science 289)

Mikulecky P, Chorvatova I. A Knowledge-Based Tools for a Scientific Program Library. Comenius University, Institute of Computer Science, 842 43 Bratislava, Czechoslovakia

Mittermeir RT, Oppitz M. Software Bases for the Flexible Composition of Application Systems. IEEE Transactions on Software Engineering April 1987 13; 4:440-460

More on Reusability (Software), System Dev. (USA) 1986 5; 11:

Morrison R, Brown AL, Carrick R, Connor RCH, Dearle A, Atkinson MP. Polymorphism Persistence and Software-Reuse in a Strongly Typed Object-Oriented Environment. Software Engineering Journal Nov 1987 2; 6:199-204

Murnan CA. Reusable Software: Trade Off Analysis and a New Approach. AD-AI59813/5 Naval Postgraduate School, June 1985

Musser DR. Aids to Hierarchical Specification Structuring and Reusing Theorems in AFFIRM-85. SIGSOFT Software Engineering Notes Aug 1985 10; 4:2-4

Myers GJ. Reliable Software through Composite Design. van Nostrand Reinhold, 1975

Neighbors J. Software Construction Using Components. PhD Thesis Tech. Report TR-160, University of California, 1980

Neighbors JM. The DRACO Approach to Constructing Software from Reusable Components. IEEE Transactions on Software Engineering 1984 10; 5:564-573

Nise NS, Griffin C. Considerations for the Design of Ada Reusable Packages. In: Proceedings 1st Conference on Ada Programming Applications for the NASA Space Station, Houston, June 1986

Nissen J, Wallis P. Portability and Style In Ada. Cambridge University Press, Cambridge, United Kingdom, 1984 (the Ada Companion Series)

Nourani GA, Jones CF. Software Reusability — A Perspective. In: Proceedings of the Eighteenth Hawaii International Conference on System Sciences. Western Periodicals Company, Honolulu, HI, USA, Jan 1985, vol 2, pp 447-456

Onuegbe EO. Software Classification as an Aid to Reuse: Initial Use as Part of a Rapid Prototyping System. In: Proceedings of 20th Hawaii International Conference on System Sciences. Hawaii Int. Conference Syst. Sci., Western Periodicals Company, Honolulu, HI, USA, 1987, vol 2, pp 521-529

Parker J, Hendley B. The Reuse of Low-Level Progamming Knowledge in the UNIVERSE Programming Environment. In: Brereton P. (ed) Software Engineering Environments. Horwood Chichester England, 1988 (Ellis Horwood books on Information Technology)

Parnas DL. On the Criteria To Be Used in Decomposing Systems Into Modules. Communications of the ACM Dec 1972 5; 12:1053-1058

Parnas DL. Designing Software for Ease of Extension and Contraction. IEEE Transactions on Software Engineering March 1979 5; 2:128-137

Parnas DL, Clement C, Weiss D. Enhancing Reusability with Information Hiding. In: Proceedings of the ITT Workshop on Reusability in Programming. Stratford, Connecticut, ITF, Newport, RI, Sept 7-9, 1983

Parnas DL, Clements PC. A Rational Design Process: How and Why to Fake It. IEEE transactions on Software Engineering Febr 1986 12; 2:251-257

Polster FJ. Reuse of Software through Partial Systems. TIB/B86-80334. Kernforschungszentrum Karlsruhe GmbH, September 1985

Pressman, Roger S. Software Engineering. McGraw-Hill, Computer Science Series, Second Edition 1987

Presson PE, Tsai J, Bowen TP, Post JV, Schmidt R. Software Inoperability and Reusability. In: Guidebook for Software Quality Measurement. Boeing Aerospace Company, Seatle, WA, July 1983

Prieto-Diaz R. A Software Classification Scheme. Technical Report 85-19 Department of Information and Computer Science, University of California, Irvine, 1985

Prieto-Diaz R, Neighbors JM. Module Interconnection Languages. Journal of System and Software Nov 1986 6; 4:307-334

Prieto-Diaz R. Domain Analysis for Reusability. COMPSAC '87 Conference. Tokyo, Japan, Oct 7-9, 1987

Prieto-Diaz R, Freeman P. Classifying Software for Reusability. IEEE Software 1987 4; 1:6-16

Prywes ED, Cheng NS, Lock TT. Use of Very High Level Languages and Program Generation by Management Professionals. IEEE Transactions on Software Engineering Sept 1984 10; 5:552-563

Przybylinksi SM. Archetyping: A Knowledge-Based Reuse Paradigm. In: Agrawal DP. (ed) Proceedings of the Workshop on Future Directions in Computer Architecture and Software; May 5-7 1986, Seabrook Island, Charlston. US Army Research Office, Research Triangle Park, NC, USA, 1986, pp 186-193

Puncello PP, Torrigiani P, Pietri F, Burion R, Cardile B, Conti M. ASPIS: A Knowledge-Based CASE Environment. IEEE Software March 1988 5; 2:58-65

Purtilo JM. Polylith Architecture. DE86007640 Illinois University March 1986

Raj RK, Levy HM. A Composition Model for Software Reuse. The Computer Journal Aug 1989 32; 4:312-322

Ramamoorthy CV, Usuda Y, Tsai W-T, Prakash A. GENESIS: An Integrated Environment for Supporting Development and Evolution of Software. IEEE 1985, pp 472-479

Ramamoorthy CV, Garg V, Prakash A. Support for Reusability in Genesis. In: Proceedings 10th Anniversary COMPSAC'86. IEEE Computer Society Press, Washington, DC, USA, Oct 1986, pp 299-305

Ratcliffe M. Report on a Workshop on Software Reuse Held at Hereford, UK on 1,2 May 1986. Software Engineering Notes Jan 1987 12; 1:42-47

Rauch-Hindin W. Reusable Software. Systems & Software, Febr 1983; 78-92

Reed N, Yeh J, Mittermeir RT, Roussopoulos R. A Programming Environment Framework Based on Reusability. International Conference on Data Engineering. IEEE Computer Society Press. Silver Spring, MD, USA, April 1984, pp 277-280

Rich C, Waters RC. Automatic Programming: Myths and Prospects. IEEE Computer Aug 1988 21; 11:40-51

Rich C, Waters RC. The Programmer's Apprentice: A Research Overview. IEEE Computer Nov 1988 21; 11:10-25

Rich C, Wills LM. Recognizing a Program's Design: A Graph-Parsing Approach. IEEE Software Jan 1990; 1:82-89

Ricket NW. Preconditions for Widespread Reuse of Code. ACM SIGSOFT Software Engineering Notes 1986 11; 2:21

Richter C, Biggerstaff T. Reusability Framework, Assessment, and Directions. In: Proceedings of 20th Hawaii International Conference on System Sciences. Hawaii

Int. Conference Syst. Sci., Honolulu, HI, USA, 1987, Western Periodicals Company, Honolulu, HI, USA, pp 502-512

Rockmore AJ. Knowledge-Based Software Turns Specifications into Efficient Programs. Electron. Des.(USA) July 1985 33; 17:105-12

Roubine O. Reusable Software. II/SA/RT.86.004 Informatique Internationale, 1984

Rouse WB, Hunt RM. Human Problems Solving in Fault Diagnoses Tasks. In: Rouse WB. (ed) Advances in Man-Machine Systems Research, vol 1. JAI Press, Greenwich, Conn., 1984

Russell GE. Experiences Implementing a Reusable Data Structure Component Taxonomy. In: Proceedings of the Joint Ada Conference, Fifth National Conference on Ada Technology and Washington Ada Symposium. U.S. Army Communications-Electronics Command, Fort Monmouth, New Jersey, 1987, pp 8-18

Schank RC. (ed) Conceptual Information Processing. Amsterdam, North-Holland, 1975, reprinted 1984 (Fundamental Studies in Computer Science vol 3)

Scherlis WL. Abstract Data Types, Specialization, and Program Reuse. In: Conradi R. et al. (ed) Advanced Programming Environments; Proceedings of an International Workshop, Trondheim, June 1986. Springer-Verlag, Berlin, Germany, 1986, pp 433-453

Selby RW. Analysing Software Reuse at the Project and Module Design Levels. In: Nickols HK, Simpson D. (eds) ESEC'87; 1st European Software Engineering Conference, Strassbourg, France, Sept 1987. Springer, Berlin, pp 227-236 (Lecture Notes in Computer Science 289)

Seppanen V. Reusability in Software Engineering. In: Freeman P. (ed) Tutorial: Software Reusability. IEEE Computer Society Press Washington, DC, 1987

Shemer I. Systems Analysis: A Systemic Analysis of a Conceptual Model. Communications of the ACM June 1987 30; 6:506-512

Shlaer S, Mellor SJ. An Object-Oriented Approach to Domain Analysis. Software Engineering Notes July 1989 14; 5:66-77

Shriver BD. Reuse Revisited: Editorial. IEEE Software Jan 1987 4; 1:5

Sivley KE. Experience and Lessons Learned in Transporting Ada Software. In: Proceedings of the Joint Ada Conference; Fifth National Conference on Ada Technology and Washington Ada Symposium. U.S. Army Communications-Electronics Command, Fort Monmouth, New Jersey, 1987, pp 436-440

Smith DD. Designing Generics for Compatibility and Reusability. In: Proceedings 1st Conference on Ada Programming Applications for the NASA Space Station. Houston, June 1986

Sneed HM, Jandrasics G. Software Recycling. In: Martin RJ. (chair) Proceedings of the Conference on Software Maintenance; Austin, Texas, September 21-24, 1987,

IEEE Computer Society Press, Washington DC, 1987

Sneed HM, Jandrasics G. Inverse Transformation from Code to Specification. In: Software Tools '89; Proceedings of the Conference held in London, June 1989. Blenheim Online, London, 1989

Soloway K, Ehrlich E. Empirical Studies of Programming Knowledge. IEEE Transactions on Software Engineering Sept 1984 10; 5:595-609

Sommerville I, Wood M. A software components catalogue. In: Davis R. (ed) Intelligent Information Systems: Progress and Prospects. Wiley 1987 pp 13-32

Spivey M. The Z Notation. Prentice-Hall, 1989

Standish TA. An Essay on Software Reuse. IEEE Transactions on Software Engineering Sept 1984 10; 5:494-497

STARS. STARS Workshop on Reusable Components of Application Software. Navel Research Laboratory, 1985

Stepoway SP, Arnold SL. The REUSE System: Cataloging and Retrieval of Reusable Software. In: Michael GA. (chair) Intellectual Leverage; Spring COMPCON 87; 32nd International Conference, San Francisco, Feb 1987, Digest of Papers. IEEE Computer Society Press Washington DC, Spring 1987, pp 376-379

Studer R. Knowledge-Based Software Engineering Environment. Comput. Phys. Commun. (Netherlands), Oct-Nov 1985 38; 2:277-87

Sugimoto H, Katoh M, Yoshida H. Logic-Based Retrieval and Reuse of Software Modules. In: Proceedings of 5th annual International Phoenix Conference on Computers and Communications. PCCC'86. IEEE Computer Society Press, Washington, DC, USA, March 1986, pp 445-449

Swanson EB, Beath CM. Maintaining Information Systems in Organizations. Wiley Chichester 1989 (John Wiley Information Systems Series)

Tajima D, Matsubara T. Inside the Japanese Software Industry. IEEE Computer 1984 17; 3:34-43

Tracz W. Software Reuse: Motivators and Inhibitors. In: Michael GA. (chair) Intellectual Leverage; Spring COMPCON 87; 32nd International Conference, San Francisco, Feb 1987, Digest of Papers. IEEE Computer Society Press Washington DC, Spring 1987, pp 358-363

Tracz W. Ada Reusability Efforts: A Survey of the State of the Practice. In: Proceedings of the Joint Ada Conference, Fifth National Conference on Ada Technology and Washington Ada Symposium. U.S. Army Communications-Electronics Command, Fort Monmouth, New Jersey, 1987, pp 35-44

Tracz W. Reusability Comes of Age. IEEE Software July 1987 4; 4:25-33

Tracz W. (ed) Software Reuse: Emerging Technology. IEEE Computer Society

Press, Washington, DC, 1988

Tracz W. Software Reuse Myths. ACM SIGSOFT, Software Engineering Notes 1988 13; 1:17-21

Truzzi O, Ghisio S. An Extended Approach to Ada Software Reusability. CSELT Tech. Rep. (Italy), vol 15, No. 1, pp 89-94, Feb 1987

Truzzi P, Ghisio S, Gouthier O. An Extended Approach to Reusability. In: Michael GA. (chair) Intellectual Leverage; Spring COMPCON 87; 32nd International Conference, San Francisco, Feb 1987, Digest of Papers. IEEE Computer Society Press Washington DC, Spring 1987, pp 385-389

Ververs F, van Katwijk J, Dusink L. Directions in Reusing Software. Report of the Faculty of Mathematics and Informatics TR 88-58, TU Delft, The Netherlands 1988

Volpano DM, Kieburtz RB. Software Templates. In: Proceedings of the 8th International Conference on Software Engineering. IEEE Computer Society Press, Los Alamitos, California, 1985, pp 55-60

Wald EE. Software Engineering with Reusable Parts. In: Michael GA. (chair) Intellectual Leverage; Spring COMPCON 87; 32nd International Conference, San Francisco, Feb 1987, Digest of Papers. IEEE Computer Society Press Washington DC, Spring 1987, pp 353-356

Ward M. Transforming a Program into a Specification. Computer Science Technical Report 88/1. School of Engineering and Applied Science. University of Durham, January 1988

Waters RC. Reuse of Cliches in the Knowledge-based Editor. In: Proceedings of an International Workshop. Springer-Verlag, Berlin, Germany, 1986, pp 536-550

Wegner P. Varieties of Reusability. In: Proceedings of the ITT Workshop on Reusability in Programming. Stratford, Connecticut, ITT, Newport, RI, September 7-9, 1983

Wegner P. Capital-intensive Software Technology. IEEE Software July 1984 1; 6:7-54

Welch PH. Parallel Processes as Reusable Components. In: Tafvelin S. (ed) Ada Components: Libraries and Tools. Proceedings of the Ada-Europe International Conference, Stockholm 26-28 May 1987. Cambridge University Press, U.K., 1987, pp 86-99 (Ada Companion Series)

Winston PH. Learning and Reasoning by Analogy. Communications of the ACM Dec 1980 23; 12:689-703

Wirfs-Brock A, Wilkerson B. Variables Limit Reusability. Journal of Object Oriented Programming May/June 1989; 38-40

Wong W. A Management Overview of Software Reuse. NBS Special Publication 500-142 U.S. Government Printing Office, Washington, DC, Sept 1986

Wood M, Sommerville I. A Knowledge-Based Software Components Catalogue. In: Brereton P. (ed) Software Engineering Environments. Horwood Chichester England, 1988 (Ellis Horwood books on Information Technology)

Woodfield SN, Embley DW, Stokes GL, Zhang K. Assumptions and Issues of Software Reusability. Proceedings of 5th annual International Phoenix Conference on Computers and Communications. PCCC'86 IEEE Computer Society Press, Washington, DC, USA, March 1986, pp 450-454

Woodfield SN, Embley DW, Scott DT. Can Programmers Reuse Software? IEEE Software July 1987 4; 4:52-59

Yamamoto S, Isoda S. SoftDA — A Reuse-Oriented Software Design System. In: Proceedings 10th Anniversary COMPSAC'86. IEEE Computer Society Press, Washington, DC, USA, Oct 1986, pp 284-290

Yeh RT, Mittermeir RT, Conceptual Modelling as a Basis for Deriving Software Requirements. In: International Computer Symposium, Taepci, Taiwan, Dec 1980

Yeh RT, Roussopoulos N, Chu B. Management of reusable software. In: The Small Computer (R)Evolution, Proceedings of COMPCON Fall 84, Sept 1984. IEEE Computer Society Press 1984, pp 311-320

Chapter 4

REDO at Oxford

P.T. Breuer
K. Lano

The Programming Research Group at Oxford University is participating in the ES-PRIT project REDO. The project is targeted at the ReEngineering and reDOcumentation of COBOL and Fortran programs. The working consortium involves academic and industrial partners across Europe, under the overall management of Lloyd's Register of Shipping in London. Three universities (Durham, Oxford and Limerick), five software products and services houses (Centrisa (Sp), CTC (Gr), ITS (Sp), Grumman (Ger), Marconi (UK)) and two large users of application codes (Electricité de France (Fr), Delft Hydraulics (Nth)) provide a lively spectrum of talents and activities.

The project as a whole aims to provide a package of tools which will modify existing programs *and* increase their maintainability. The project design is directed towards three main goals:

- Programs must be restructured to support maintainability properties.

- Documentation must be adduced and kept in line with code

- Features related to the validation of code must be incorporated and enhanced

Oxford is heavily involved in the latter area, whilst the specialist applied software houses concentrate on the restructuring of control and data flow (Grumman), and the separation of environmental dependencies (Centrisa, Delft). The Centre for Software Maintenance at Durham is cooperating with ITS on the generation and maintenance of code documentation.

The Programming Research Group at Oxford is contributing expertise in formal methods to the project as a whole. In particular, the Oxford-developed specification language "Z" is being exploited in various parts of the programme. The Programming Research Group is cooperating with the University of Limerick in the design of an Intermediate Language for the representation of Fortran and COBOL code. Whilst Limerick contributes experience of application codes in formulating the top levels of the language, Oxford contributes knowledge of abstract language models to the design of the lower level, making sure that all the language constructs can be expressed in terms of a simple few, which are completely specified in Z.

The resulting language, "Uniform", is intended to capture relatively low-level features of application codes; those which are common in large COBOL and Fortran programs, but provision is made for the expression of high level design ideas. The language is based on a simple version of the object-oriented paradigm, and models applications as sets of processes which pass low-level structures to each other by way of a substrate of multi-purpose queues. The detail of the language mimics the overall operational semantics of Fortran and COBOL rather than interrupt-driven semantics, however, in that each process must demand its own messages from its input queues, and cannot be activated externally. Indeed, a degree of explicitly non-deterministic behaviour may be directly expressed in the language, commensurate with the indeterminism commonly encountered in multi-process accesses to global data which is updated by a single process.

The REDO toolkit will operate by translating COBOL and Fortran codes into Uniform, then remodelling the Uniform code before retranslating into the source language again. Along the way, the environmental and user-interface dependencies will be separated out into a design database, and this information will be kept in alignment with the transformed code. The intermediate language contains explicit constructs which express iteration over the elements of a data structure such as a file, array or queue, and constructs like these are intended to aid the restructuring process. It is a pity that more such high level abstractions cannot be incorporated into the language, but the design is constrained by the immediate needs of the partners involved in restructuring and translating COBOL and Fortran codes, and cannot contain over-speculative features. Most programming abstractions will be expressed as generic process types, and not through built-in syntax.

Below we give descriptions of the technical basis of our reverse-engineering processes; these are concerned with the derivation of mathematical and abstract descriptions from code that has already been cleaned up and restructured according to metrics that measure the modularisation and quality of the application from an object-orientated point of view. That is, how well the application is factored into procedures and operations on certain abstract data types, with the number of low-level accesses to such structures minimised. Standard examples of the implicit use of abstract data types in COBOL, include the use of files to implement relations, along with the usual relational operations of projection, deletion and extension.

4.1   THE ABSTRACT REPRESENTATION OF CODE

The meaning of a piece of code will be expressed as a specification $v_1', \ldots, v_n'$, with v_i' representing the value of v_i after execution of the command, v_i the value before. These specifications have a semantics [5], in terms of the usual *weakest precondition* predicate transformer semantics wp [3]:

$$wp(\vec{v} : \theta, \ \psi) \ \equiv \ \forall \vec{v}' \cdot (\theta \Rightarrow \psi')$$

for all ψ in the set Ω^V of predicates with the free variables $\vec{v}$.

We can prove by induction that all commands of the UNIFORM language ([6]) can be expressed as such predicates, in the sense that for each command C, there is a *characteristic predicate*, θ_C, which can be obtained from the characteristic predicates of the syntactic subcommands of C, and which has the property:

$$\forall \psi \in \Omega^V \cdot (wp(\vec{v} : \theta_C, \ \psi) \ = \ wp(C, \ \psi))$$

with wp for commands being defined in a standard way [1].

The aspects of this conversion which contribute to the comprehension of the functionality of the code lie with the expression of message-passing commands and concurrently executing processes. Because UNIFORM does not have an "ALT" construct capable of making a control flow decision based upon which of several queues become ready for communication first (as found in OCCAM or Ada), we are able to represent processes as functions or relations on (potentially) infinite sequences; the process is a transformation of histories of communications on its input queues to histories of communications on its output queues. Following the approach pioneered by the GYPSY [2] system, we consider the significant points in the execution of a process to be: (i) initiation, (ii) arrival at a message-passing statement (and hence at a point of potential suspension), and (iii) termination. We only need to discover the effect of the process at these points. This will be considered in detail below.

4.2 THE METHOD

4.2.1 Mathematical Expression of Types

The type structures included in the UNIFORM language encompass the usual array and record structures as used in PASCAL (although without recursive data types), plus file structures able to support the file operations used in COBOL, such as accessing a record in a file by referring to a value of a key field of a record. All of these data structures can be represented mathematically as functions or special record structures, and it is these representations that are then used in proving properties of programs.

4.2.2 The Expression of Commands

Basic Commands.

Simple assignments and conditionals can be translated into specifications directly, without analysis of the meaning of the code; a concurrent assignment

$$\vec{v} \ \vec{s} := \vec{e}$$

becomes simply

$$v_1' = rep(v_1, s_1, e_1) \wedge \ldots \wedge v_n' = rep(v_n, s_n, e_n)$$

Where $rep(x, i, a)$ (here with $x = v_k$, $i = s_k$, $a = e_k$) yields the expression produced by replacing the contents of the given variable x i by a, where x is an identifier, i is a selector expression (a sequence of array/file references or record field selections), and a is an expression. This is defined by recursion on the structure of the selector. That is, an assignment to a component of a complex variable is represented logically as an update of the whole structure as a single object. A conditional

  IF E THEN $c1$ ELSE $c2$ END IF

becomes $(E \Rightarrow \theta_1) \wedge (\neg E \Rightarrow \theta_2)$ if θ_1 expresses $c1$, θ_2 expresses $c2$.
  Similarly, if θ_1 expresses $c1$ and θ_2 expresses $c2$ then

$$\exists \vec{w} \cdot \theta_1[\vec{w}/\vec{v}'] \wedge \theta_2[\vec{w}/\vec{v}]$$

expresses the sequential construct $c1; c2$.

Loops.

The difficulty, as with validation, comes in determining the effect of loops, particularly unbounded loops, DO WHILE or DO UNTIL constructs.

It is possible to automatically obtain an expression of such loops as recursive functions, but this may not be of practical assistance in simplifying the description. Instead we look for a concise and expressive description of what the loop achieves; by using heuristics we try to discover suitably strong *invariants* of the loop, that is, a predicate Inv of the variables of a loop DO WHILE E : C END DO such that $E \wedge Inv \Rightarrow wp(C, Inv)$ (this is also written $\{Inv \wedge E\}\ C\ \{Inv\}$).

Heuristics and Discovery.

We use heuristics adapted from Gries [3] to generate invariants for an existing loop command. These have been used successfully in the automatic documentation and verification of PASCAL programs.

If all heuristics fail, we denote the effect of the loop by some (new) arbitrary relation $r_L(\vec{v})$ of the program variables, and give an implicit definition of the loop effect by asserting that the properties

$$\forall \vec{v}\ (r_L(\vec{v}) \wedge \neg E \Rightarrow R)$$
$$\forall \vec{v}\ (r_L(\vec{v}) \wedge E \Rightarrow wp(C, r_L(\vec{v})))$$

hold of r_L (where R is the desired postcondition, which may also involve relations representing other loops). Additional (initial) conditions on r_L emerge as proof obligations generated by tracing back through the program, having assumed $r_L(\vec{v})$ as the precondition of the loop. The least (in the usual denotational semantics sense of least defined) solution of these requirements provides us with the strongest definition of the effect of the loop. The r_L given by this solution will imply the r_L' obtained from any other solution, but it may be expressed as 'the least r such that ...', and from this an explicit form must be deduced.

Note that we try to reduce bounded loops to multiple or single assignments; for instance a loop that updates an array or file, with different iterations of the loop using different indices, can be written as a single functional override (see example one below).

Dealing with Concurrency and Message-Passing.

The form of concurrency adopted in the UNIFORM language is message-passing with both blocking and non-blocking semantics; processes can execute in parallel, communicating only via message streams (queues), and without reference to a global clock. Characteristic assertions about processes need only mention those variables that are externally visible, these are the queues (more accurately the queue histories), since in the "clean" version of the language there are no global variables.

Viewing RECEIVE and SEND commands as transformations on buffer histories (represented by new variables $b_{in,p}$ for the total sequence of messages received along b by process instance p, and $b_{out,p}$ for the total sequence of messages output along b by p), we can define

$$wp(\text{SEND } x \text{ TO } b,\ R) = R[b_{out,p} \frown \langle x \rangle\ /\ b_{out,p}]$$
$$wp(\text{RECEIVE } x \text{ FROM } b,\ R) = \forall \nu \cdot R[\nu/x\ \ b_{in,p} \frown \langle \nu \rangle\ /\ b_{in,p}]$$

representing the fact that the value of the next item to be received from the queue is unknown. This command can be expressed by the predicate

$$\exists \nu \cdot (x' = \nu \ \wedge \ b'_{in,p} = b_{in,p} \ ^\frown \langle \nu \rangle)$$

where ν is a variable new to the program. Notice that we have no knowledge of *when* the attempt to receive a message will block; as we have no knowledge of the global state of the message queue from within a particular process — unless the queue is in both the SEND and RECEIVE lists of the process. As each queue b can be used by at most two processes, say p sending to b and q receiving from b, we can however assert that

$$b_{out,p} = b_{in,q} \ ^\frown b$$

(The actual contents of the queue b is the remainder — tail — of the total sequence of messages sent to b after the total sequence of messages received from b has been removed) is a global invariant of the program. To determine the effect of a process p, we place assertions

$$\{\textbf{prove}: \ \theta(\vec{ins}, \vec{outs})\}$$

immediately prior to each RECEIVE x FROM ms command in the process body, and, if the process can terminate, at the end of the code of the process. The predicate θ stands for the yet-to-be-determined effect of the process.

We then work back from these requirements to deduce what properties are needed for this predicate θ that expresses the process behaviour, and hence we can deduce its properties by examining the proof obligations generated by the code.

We are assuming for simplicity that all queues are unbounded, but if it were possible for queues to block on send, then we would also need to check the process behaviour at the points of execution when a SEND statement has just been reached. In practice we associate a new relation r_S with each significant point S in the process execution, and use the verification/reverse-engineering techniques to find out more information about this relation. The visible behaviour of the process is just the disjunction of these relations; and the behaviour of the process when it is actually blocked is the disjunction

$$(r_{S_1}(\vec{v}) \wedge \neg \ enabled(S_1)) \ \vee \dots \vee \ (r_{S_n}(\vec{v}) \wedge \neg \ enabled(S_n))$$
$$\vee \ (terminated(p) \wedge r_T(\vec{v}))$$

where $terminated(p)$ characterises the states in which the process can be terminated, $enabled(S_i)$ is the condition that the message statement immediately following the execution point S_i can proceed (it is $b \neq \langle \ \rangle$ for a RECEIVE command on b for instance).

Combining the Effect of Several Processes.

Processes can be connected "in series", with the output of one process forming the input to another, or in a cyclic arrangement, with the output of a process being returned to one of its inputs via another process.

We can define the overall effect of such networks from the effects of the individual processes: composition in series of process instances $id1$, $id2$, $id1$ supplying input to $id2$ via the channel b, has characteristic formula

$$\exists\, b\ (\theta_{id1}(\vec{a}, b) \wedge \theta_{id2}(b, \vec{c}))$$

Where b is not in the list $\vec{a}$ or list $\vec{c}$, and these two lists are disjoint.

If processes form a circuit of communications then, if they are all functional, the meaning of the combination of the processes can be determined by using fixed points; as in the analysis of Kahn networks [4], or the semantics of LUCID. For instance, in the simple case of feedback from the output of one process into one of its inputs via another process:

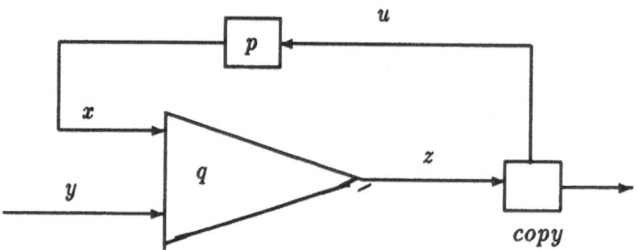

Where q transforms inputs x and y into z, which is copied onto two streams, one of which is the final output, and the other returns to the input of q after transformation via p. This arrangement can be expressed by a recursive equation:

$$z = q(x, y) \quad where \quad x = p(q(x, y))$$

Functional networks can always be reduced to a sequence of equations possibly involving mutual recursion. In UNIFORM, since each queue can have at most one process writing to it, and at most one reading from it, we must put in explicit *copy* processes if we wish two processes to read from a single queue, and (deterministic) merge processes to combine two streams into one.

4.3 EXAMPLES

4.3.1 Finding Prime Numbers

The following example demonstrates the benefits of transforming source code into mathematical representations in order to improve comprehensibility and verifiability. The program:

```
max: NUMERIC VALUE 2000;
TableOfPrimes CONTAINS max OCCURRENCES OF BOOL
              SELECTABLE BY INDEX;
pp: TableOfPrimes;
I : INTEGER;
Subrange VALUES ARE <2,..,max>;
dp: Subrange
```

```
BEGIN
  DO VARYING I FOR EACH INDEX IN <1,..,max> : pp(I) := true
  END DO;
  dp := 2;
  DO WHILE dp < max:
      DO VARYING I FROM dp + dp TO max BY dp: pp(I) := false
      END DO;
      DO VARYING I FOR EACH INDEX IN <dp + 1,..,max> UNTIL pp(I):
      END DO;
      dp := I
  END DO
END
```

is intended to derive all the primes between 1 and *max* by the well-known "sieve" method. We can analyse this program more clearly if we write it as:

$$max : \mathsf{N}$$
$$\overline{max = 2000}$$

$$TableOfPrimes == 1 .. 2000 \rightarrow Bool$$

$$pp : TableOfPrimes$$
$$I \; : \mathsf{Z}$$
$$dp : 2 .. max$$

BEGIN
$pp := \{j : 1 .. max \cdot (j, true)\};$
$I, dp := max, 2;$
DO WHILE $(dp < max)$:
$\qquad pp := pp \oplus \{j : 2 * dp .. max | dp \; divides \; j \cdot (j, false)\};$
$\qquad dp := \mu \; j : dp + 1 .. max \cdot pp(j)$
END DO
END

and we can eliminate the variable I and the statement $I := max$, so reducing the complexity of the description, in addition we have only one loop in this version, as opposed to four in the original description, with two of these nested within another.

4.3.2 Fibonacci Function

We can write a distributed program based on processes $\{p1, copy, sum, next\}$ which computes the Fibonacci sequence $1, 1, 2, 3, 5, 8, \ldots$ in UNIFORM:

```
p1:                              copy:
  SEND 1 TO x;                     DO WHILE true:
  SEND 1 TO x;                       RECEIVE a FROM x;
  DO WHILE true:                     SEND a TO s;
    RECEIVE a FROM z;                SEND a TO t
    SEND a TO x                    END DO
  END DO
```

```
sum:                                     next:
  DO WHILE true:                           RECEIVE a FROM t;
    RECEIVE a FROM s;                      DO WHILE true:
    RECEIVE b FROM y;                        RECEIVE a FROM t;
    SEND a+b TO z                            SEND a TO y
  END DO                                   END DO
```

From these processes we can write down equations connecting the input and output histories of each message stream:

$$z_{out} = sum(s_{in}, y_{in})$$
$$s_{out} = t_{out} = x_{in}$$
$$y_{out} = tail(t_{in})$$
$$x_{out} = \langle 1,1 \rangle ^\frown z_{in}$$

Which, if we identify the (total sequence of) outputs to a queue and inputs from a queue, can be reduced to equations:

$$z \;\; = sum(\textit{fib}, tail(\textit{fib}))$$
$$\textit{fib} = \langle 1,1 \rangle ^\frown z$$

which has solution $\textit{fib}$ = the Fibonacci sequence, by an easy induction. This is an example of where the effect of an apparently obscure program can be derived more easily by using predicates than by using low-level code transformations. Applying such transformations in this case is difficult because it cannot be assumed that all the queues are of "0-length", that is, are synchronised message-passing mechanisms, as the queue s must be able to buffer at least one element. This is clear from the specification (since $\#s_{in} = \#y_{in}$ at the beginning of the while loop in sum, but $\#s_{out} = \#y_{out} + 1$, so $\#s \geq 1$ by the global invariants); but isn't so clear from the raw code.

4.4   OTHER APPROACHES

We have also pursued an approach based on the transformation of code into functional specifications. These consist of a set of

- top-level function definitions of the form *lhs* = *rhs*, each guarded by ...

- a predicate defining the valid domain elements, and each dependent on ...

- a set of lower-level local specifications.

The initial specification generated is not particularly "human-readable", but we have found that the application of a few relatively simple automatic transformations produces a surprisingly acceptable form. This can then serve as the basis for more strictly selected transformations. The automatic transformations we use are:

Promotion: designated *lhs* entities are promoted to top-level by renaming if necessary (usually function entities are derived from distinct labels in the source code, and are therefore already distinct).

Elimination: all lower-level entities are eliminated by substituting their specifications in the higher-level specifications which use them.

Normalisation: redundancies such as a projection operation applied to a tuple are removed. Specifications with expressions on their *rhs* which consist of disjoint cases are converted instead into guarded specifications and simple expressions.

For example the following program:

```
INTEGER STACK s;
INTEGER FUNCTION ra(m, n) IS RETURN(n) FROM
BEGIN
        IF (m = 0)
        THEN    IF (empty(s))
                THEN    n := n + 1;
                ELSE    RECEIVE m FROM s;
                        n := ra(m − 1, n + 1);
                END IF;
        ELSE    IF (n = 0)
                THEN    n := ra(m − 1, 1);
                ELSE    SEND m TO s;
                        n := ra(m, n − 1);
                END IF;
        END IF;
END
```

transforms automatically to the following normalised specification:

$$
\begin{array}{llll}
ra(m, n, s) & = & n + 1, & \text{if } (m = 0 \wedge empty(s)) \\
ra(m, n, v : s) & = & ra(v - 1, n + 1, s), & \text{if } (m = 0) \\
ra(m, n, s) & = & ra(m - 1, 1, s), & \text{if } (n = 0) \\
ra(m, n, s) & = & ra(m, n - 1, m : s), & \text{otherwise}
\end{array}
$$

Once it is in this state, we can apply a transformation which replaces the explicit stack manipulation by continuation-passing. We get the specification:

$$
\begin{array}{llll}
ra(m, n, [\,]) & = & ra'(m, n, g) \text{ where } g(n) = n + 1 \\
ra'(m, n, c) & = & c(n + 1), & \text{if } (m = 0) \\
ra'(m, n, c) & = & ra'(m - 1, 1, c), & \text{if } (n = 0) \\
ra'(m, n, c) & = & ra'(m, n - 1, c'), & \text{otherwise} \\
& & \text{where } c'(n) = ra'(m - 1, n, c)
\end{array}
$$

The general transformation into continuation programming which we have applied here takes the form

$$
\begin{array}{llllll}
f(p_0, [\,]) & = & g(p_0) & f(x, [\,]) & = & f'(x, g), \\
f(p_0, v : s) & = & f(h(p_0, v), s) & f'(p_0, c) & = & c(p_0) \\
f(p_1, s) & = & f(k(p_1), l(p_1) : s) & f'(p_1, c) & = & f'(k(p_1), c') \\
& & & & & \text{where } c'(x) = f'(h(x, l(p_1)), c)
\end{array}
$$

Now, we can reason that all "reasonable" continuation programs are derived as

$$
f(x, c) = c(f_0(x))
$$

for some more basic function f_0. Applying this reasoning to ra' above and eliminating c' by substituting its definition in the specification above, we get $ra(m, n, [\ ]) = ra_0(m, n) + 1$, where

$$
\begin{aligned}
ra_0(m, n) &= n, & if\ (m = 0)\\
ra_0(m, n) &= ra_0(m - 1, 1), & if\ (n = 0)\\
ra_0(m, n) &= ra_0(m - 1, ra_0(m, n - 1)), & otherwise
\end{aligned}
$$

which tells us that $ra(m, n, [\ ])$ is essentially the Ackerman function.

4.5   CONCLUSION

The methods described above apply verification techniques to the reverse-engineering of a particular concurrent programming language; the process of deriving and simplifying a mathematical description of a piece of code is very similar to the process of trying to prove that its behaviour satisfies a particular specification, the difference being that in reverse-engineering we are producing and refining our specification as we progress. The documentation produced by this system can be used as input for theorem-proving and interface validation tools, and could be used as the basis of a translation of the code into a functional programming language, or for further refinement of the specifications to meet new requirements (reverse-engineering). We argue that the mathematical description of the code is a useful step towards a more concise and easily comprehended description of a program, and so this process improves maintenance and re-use possibilities for applications.

References

[1] An Axiomatic Semantics for UNIFORM. REDO Document TN-PRG-1011

[2] Good D. Mechanical Proofs About Computer Programs. In: Rich C, Waters C. (eds) Artificial Intelligence and Software Engineering. Morgan Korfmann Ltd, 1984

[3] Gries D. The Science of Programming. Springer-Verlag, 1981

[4] Kahn G. The Semantics of a Simple Language for Parallel Programming. In: Information Processing 74. North-Holland Amsterdam, 1974, pp 471- 475

[5] Morgan C. et al. On the Refinement Calculus. PRG-70 Technical Monograph 1988

[6] UNIFORM: A Language Geared to System Description and Transformation. REDO (ESPRIT 2 Project P2487) document TN-NIL-1002

Chapter 5

Sharing for Quality

C. Bron
E.J. Dijkstra

5.1   INTRODUCTION

Our position on software re-use is based on an experience over the past 10 years with the design, implementation and use of a programming language (Modular Pascal) [3] for (large scale) systems projects. This language, a superset of Pascal, was designed for the purpose of systems programming, with emphasis on the possibility of *language extension* by the use of libraries of modules. Eg. the concept of parallel processes and synchronisation, is completely implemented as a library module. Built-in extensions are: the module concept, open array parameters, exception handling, and, for systems programming, in-line code (or assembly) statements and type-conversion.

5.2   SHARING AS A MEANS TO AVOID DUPLICATION

Rather than putting an emphasis on *re-use* we have tended to stress the concept of sharing, re-use being just a form of sharing. Sharing as such is — of course — not of interest, but its corollary: the avoidance of duplication. Duplication is encountered at many levels of the software process:

- duplication of bits of code, as is usually done by linkers;

- duplication of files (sometimes this can be avoided, eg. by the Unix file-linking mechanism);

- duplication of core-images, as eg. in the Unix fork mechanism, or when non-sharable program code is loaded;

- duplication of (parts of) code files during compilation, especially in the case of library supplied include files;

- duplication of source code (in some forms called: code grabbing), making small changes to the original; (Some language features practically enforce this, cf. the adaptation of constants used in Pascal array-bounds, to comply with the rigid type system.)

- and finally (coming to the crux of the re-use issue): duplication of human effort in rewriting (and documenting, testing, etc.) software which — in essence — has been written before, and should or could be part of a software library.

In the course of this 10-year period we have been involved in various ways with the design of methods and mechanisms that avoid any of the above forms of duplication. The methods and mechanisms for (code) sharing are found on several levels:

- operating system level, especially concerning linking and the RUN mechanism;

- language level, especially: parameterisation, extension, and robustness;

- human level, eg. design issues.

Let us first give a few examples at the low end of the spectrum and finish by a slightly more detailed exposé of the re-use-component (the human effort).

5.3   TECHNIQUES TO PROMOTE SHARING

5.3.1   Implementation Level

In the SUPOS/MUPOS family of Operating Systems, there was only a single compiled copy of any module on disk, and the system loaded a module's code into memory on demand. Thus, the code space of the system formed an unlimited virtual memory, supported by the file system. The RUN/FORK mechanism [7] was based on sharing of code and data between the running program and the program to be RUN on top of that (as a procedure). The running program then served as a library for the program to be RUN. That program was *dynamically linked* to this already running library. This could proceed in a nested fashion. Sharing of data basically followed the access-path along the process-hierarchy down to the root of the initial operating system, as far as allowed by the module-induced block structure. Code was shared globally, ie. also between parallel branches of the process hierarchy.

In our current implementations, based on existing Operating Systems, we once more strive for optimal sharing. Library modules are not linked into application programs, but can be loaded separately, after which an application is run (dynamically linked) sharing the underlying library. This can proceed in nested fashion, as in MUPOS/SUPOS.

5.3.2   Language Level

The important issues at the language level are parameterisation, extension and robustness.

Parametrisation.

As for parameterisability, we mention one important but often neglected technique: the use of procedural parameters. These are vital in isolating application dependencies from the algorithmic body, eg. in

```
PROCEDURE sort_array (lo, hi: integer;
                      FUNCTION before (i, j: integer): boolean;
                      PROCEDURE swap (i, j: integer));
```

The two actual procedures for **before** and **swap** have to be supplied by the application environment. Only here knowledge of the type of array elements is embedded. i and j are only indices. In this case, the algorithm "sort" is parametrised with an abstract data type with two operations.

For this technique to work properly, the language must allow the use of locally declared procedures (otherwise, only global arrays, and not even parameters, might be sorted), to be passed as parameters. (Many languages do not have locally declared procedures. Modula-2 allows local procedure declarations, but these procedures may not be passed as parameters.)

Extension.

The second aspect, extension, is closely related to the concept of inheritance in object oriented languages, and the idea of class prefixing in Simula67. Its basic principle consists of the idea that at times a conversion in interpretation is possible between a record and its first field (they share the same address) and in *this* sense the first field is privileged. Thus any record having as its first field a pointer to another record with the same property can be part of a list, and thus list-operations can be written just once for all linked records.

Robustness.

The importance of the third aspect, robustness, stems from the fact that the implementor of a library module cannot control the (ab)use of the module: virtually no assumptions can be made about the way in which modules are going to be embedded into applications. The *exception* mechanism can be used to enforce robustness of a library procedure: when its precondition is not fulfilled, it signals an exception. In this way, the postcondition for abuse is **false**, as it should be.

5.4   THE HUMAN FACTOR IN SHARING

The projects we have been working on provided an ideal experimental environment for software re-use. We found that a factor which is at least as important as the saving in human effort is the increased correctness, reliability and robustness that is obtained when "design for re-use" and "re-use" are both practiced.

Reliability of re-usable modules and reliability of the applications in which these are used increases because

- it is impossible to make the same mistake more than once;

- if no assumptions can be made about the way in which a module is going to be used, the robustness will be an integral part of the design;

- the amount of effort invested in the (correct) design and implementation of re-usable modules is definitively greater if it is known that the effort is not for a single shot application;

- modules being re-used are "exercised" more frequently, and commonly not (just) by their designer which makes the probability of the discovery of remaining flaws higher, and convergence into stability faster.

5.5 IDENTIFYING AREAS OF RE-USE

Our experience with re-use and design for re-use has not been "domain oriented". This can be understood since it was collected during the development of Operating Systems. We found that even in these areas many algorithms and data types can be encapsulated for re-use [5]. We briefly mention some of these:

- sorting and searching

- manipulation and transformation of file names

- data structures like trees and lists

- handling of wildcard file names

- conversion of numerical values into character sequences and vice versa

- command line handling (compulsory and optional arguments), and default settings

- the scanning of search paths (in a file system)

- tree structured scanning of directories

Without going into further details, we mention that many of the above operations are often included in an operating system. In the ModPas environments, modules providing these functions are equally available (and shared with the Operating System) at the application development level.

5.6 DESIGN FOR RE-USE

A difficult matter is the *design* of library modules. In the case of array sorting there is not much of a problem, one might say any data type has the property "sortable" if it can provide the two operations (**before** and **swap**) with the intended semantics (total ordering, and the interchange of i and j in pre- and postconditions). A candidate for extension of the concept of sortable would be a binary search. Usually, such modules can best be thought of as abstract data types.

In many other cases, the design is not so straightforward, and very careful considerations and sometimes several iterations are necessary before a module takes on a satisfactory form. We briefly mention some of the relevant aspects:

- choice of operations

- choice of parameters: their order, naming, mnemonics, standards.

- level of abstraction. A very low level results in a low re-use efficiency; a high level results in a smaller application domain. Another consequence of a wrong level of abstraction may be an unacceptable loss of efficiency.

- information hiding. Hiding implementation details makes re-use of the interface in other contexts possible (portability). But this also may preclude the extension of the module. In some cases, eg. in our string handling module [3], we have decided not to hide the implementation: additional string operations can now be made outside the module (extension) without losing efficiency.

- sometimes modules only come into existence after recognition of the potential for re-use by first making — in different environments — a number of designs, that turn out to be so similar that they are later unified into a single library module.

- modesty of design. Ie. can a limited module be extended to provide more functionality if required, or should it provide the full scale to begin with?

An example of what *we* consider a satisfactory interface can be found in [3]. Some of the answers to the above questions have been transformed into "rules of thumb", but we are still fully in the process of learning.

5.7 ADAPTATION OF INTERFACES

However well designed interfaces may be, there will be occasions where an interface must be changed. In Modular Pascal an interface is fully determined by the exports of a module. Two compiled modules can cooperate if there is an *exact* match between the (exported) interface and the interface that was valid for that module when the importing module was compiled [8]. This is actually a stricter requirement than necessary. Cooperation should be possible if the exporting module provides what the importing module needs. In other words, a library module might show as many (inter)faces as there are clients. Extension of the interface of a library module should never do any harm, contraction or alteration might or might not, depending on the community of users. This problem was also raised by [6] who was — understandably — very dissatisfied with Modula-2 in retrospect. Here we also encounter a *disadvantage* of sharing: if library modules are not shared, but linked into an application, that application will not be sensitive to subsequent changes in the library module's interface. On the other hand, shared modules that are "improved" (without an interface change) are instantaneously updated in all applications. A more flexible scheme for interface checking would necessitate the availability of highly "intelligent" linkers and/or loaders that have much of the compiler's symbol table and type information at their disposal.

References

[1] Bron C. Modules, Program Structures and the Structuring of Operating Systems. In: Duyvestijn AJW, Lockemann PC. Trends in Information Processing Systems; 3rd Conference, Munich. Springer, 1981 (Lecture Notes in Computer Science no. 123)

[2] Bron C, Dijkstra EJ. A Note on the Checking of Interfaces between Independently Compiled Modules. SIGPLAN Notices 1985 20; 8:60-63

[3] Bron C, Dijkstra EJ. Report on the Programming Language Modular Pascal. University of Groningen, 3rd edition, 1989

[4] Bron C, Dijkstra EJ. Toward Libraries of Reusable Modules. Technical Report CS 8901, University of Groningen, 1989

[5] Bron C, Dijkstra EJ. A Better Way to Combine Efficient String Length Encoding and Zero Termination. SIGPLAN Notices 1989 6; 24:11-19

[6] Gutknecht J. Variations on the Role of Module Interfaces. Structured Programming 1989 1; 10:40-46

Chapter 6

The MERLIN Approach to the Re-use of Software Components

Joachim Cramer
Heike Hünnekens
Wilhelm Schäfer
Stefan Wolf

6.1 INTRODUCTION

Some of many hard problems in current software production include the lack of proper organisational and tool supported models to manage large scale software production, the lack of integrated tools based on well-defined and commonly agreed integration mechanisms as well as the lack of formally based methods to allow to properly defined later re-usable software components [1]

In order to overcome these (and maybe also some other) deficits, a number of major efforts have been formed around the world (eg. SWB [40], ESF ([48], [26], ARCADIA [5], etc). The basic idea is to support software production by an integrated tool set in a more industrialised style which is emphasised by using the term software factory for such a tool set. Two key issues of this approach are:

1. producing software according to a precisely defined software process model (eg. [21], [43], [25], [39]), and

2. re-using prefabricated software components (eg. [42], [33], [53]).

These two key issues are also the main concern of the research project MERLIN carried out at the Software Technology Center in Dortmund in collaboration with the University of Dortmund since 1988. Part of this work is funded by the German Ministry for Research (BMFT) under the Eureka project ESF (Grant-No. ITS 8802). The MERLIN ideas and results in the process modeling area have been described in [16], [34], and [17]. The aim of this paper is to summarise the MERLIN approach towards the re-use of (software) components as presented in [13].

The approach can be classified as a compositional approach [6] to the planned re-use of software components. We prefer the compositional approach to re-use, as the generation approach can be applied only to very narrow application domains. In order to attack the re-use of software components in a planned manner, the activities involved in the re-use of software components have to be an integral part of the software process. We therefore try to tackle the re-use problem by giving a process-oriented view on re-use describing the particularly necessary re-use-related activities as well as the relations between them. We call this coherent view on re-use

---

[1]The term software component not only means source or object code fragments, but fragments of all other types of documents produced during a software process like fragments of a requirements specification, design, ... of all (or at least many) different types.

the software re-use process. This software re-use process is independent of the different types of possible re-usable software components like (parts of) a requirements document, a design document or source code. Therefore the software re-use process can be applied to the development and re-use of any of these components irrespective of their type. On a high abstraction level the whole software re-use process can be subdivided into the processes of producing and re-using re-usable software components.

The aim of the process of producing is to populate a library with a mass of re-usable software components. It therefore covers the development of software components, the certification of those components as re-usable ones, and their classification according to functional or non-functional characteristics in order to store them in a library.

The re-usable software components stored in the library are then re-used by applying the process of re-using. The first activity to be carried out in that process is the retrieval of a software component which best meets the users needs. As a retrieved component can rarely be re-used as it is, it has to be adapted by a modification of (parts of) it. By performing the integration activity the adapted component becomes part of a specific software system.

6.2   THE ACTIVITIES OF THE SOFTWARE PROCESS

In the following sections we consider the activities of the software re-use process in more detail. Although we consider all activities, the emphasis is put on the activities development, classification and retrieval. This emphasis reflects the background for our work as well as our opinion that these are the topics where the conventional technologies lack at most so that more fundamental research has to take place.

6.2.1   Development

The development activity of the software re-use process aims at populating the library with re-usable software components. This activity can either take place before the software re-use process has been instantiated in order to provide a critical mass of re-usable software components or it can take place after the software re-use process has been instantiated during a running software development process. The development of a critical mass of components before the first instantiation of the software re-use process is inevitable as the mass of components is part of the original capital of a viable re-use environment. This critical mass of re-usable software components can be developed from scratch and/or it can be collected by studying the huge mass of already produced software components. In the latter case components are identified which can be generalised into an abstraction which is potentially re-usable (re-engineering). Although the first way is more likely to succeed, the second one is also important as it is sometimes the only economical one [23]. In both cases there are some key issues to be tackled which heavily influence the ability to re-use the developed software components. These key issues are:

- the software component model, ie. the principles and concepts the software components have to adhere to,

- the notations, ie. the formalisms used for describing the software components according to the software component model,

- the development method, ie. the way in which the notations are used to describe the software components, and

- the development tools, ie. the software which supports the development of re-usable software components.

On the one hand, if software components are a priori developed for re-use, one would choose notations for their description which are based on software engineering principles like modularisation which foster re-use.

On the other hand, most of the existing software components are typically written in notations like FORTRAN or COBOL, which are not or only partially based on those principles. If a posteriori such software components should be re-used, one can either try to restructure the description in the originally used notation or one can transform the description of those components into a notation which is based on those principles as investigated eg. in [4] and [14].

In all cases the definition of a sound software component model and its corresponding notation are a key issue. However, a language in itself can only provide means for describing re-usable software components but it can not guarantee by its syntactical definition that the notation is really applied. For example, on one hand it is possible to write re-usable code using programming languages which do not provide notational support for the principles which foster re-use. On the other hand it is possible to write not re-usable code using programming languages which provide notational support. Therefore, although a language greatly influences a person's re-use mind set and how software engineers develop re-usable abstractions [56], there is a need for development methods which guide software developers in using a notation in such a way that the resulting software components are re-usable. It depends on the notational support for the principles which foster re-use how complex such a development method has to be. That is, while for some notations few guidelines are sufficient, for others all of the principles which foster re-use have to be a posteriori introduced into the use of a notation via a huge number of guidelines.

The development of software components in a given notation has then to follow the determined guidelines and it has to be assured that the developed components adhere to them. This is a precondition for classifying a developed software component as re-usable. It can be partially done in a constructive manner by appropriate tools which provide support for the development of re-usable software components. If these key issues have been tackled, the content of the re-use library evolves after the instantiation of the software re-use process through the development of re-usable software components during running software development processes. In order to achieve that, the single project view of the software development process has to be given up, as the development of re-usable software components costs extra effort which has to be amortised by its later re-use within other projects [55].

Software Component Model.

The effort needed to re-use a software component depends on general software engineering principles for the structuring of software components which can be applied to nearly all kinds of software components [2].

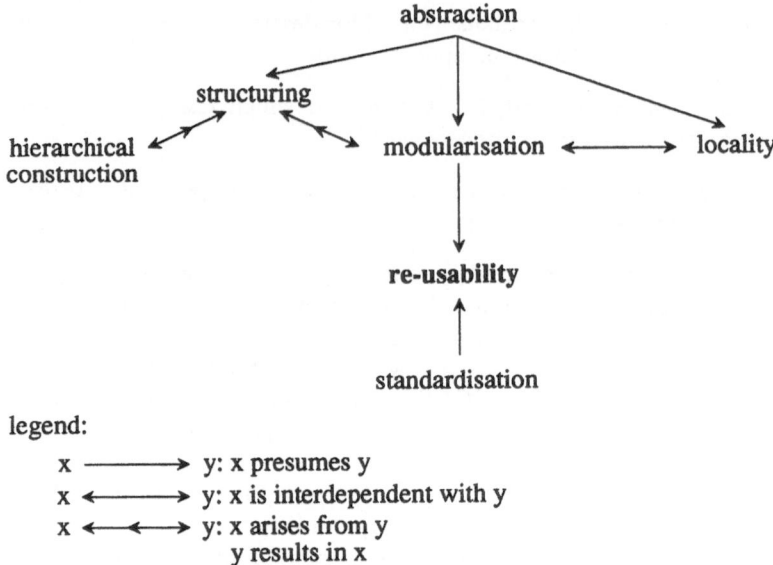

legend:

x ⟶ y: x presumes y
x ⟷ y: x is interdependent with y
x ⟵⟷ y: x arises from y
        y results in x

Figure 6.1: Principles which Foster Re-use

When strictly applying these principles, the developed software component exhibits the properties of a re-usable software component like its usability in the sense that the software component is portable, reliable and user friendly, as well as its maintainability in the sense that the software component is easily testable, understandable and modifiable [2]. In any case, the application of these principles to software components of any types fosters their later re-use. Therefore, to provide a uniform framework for the re-use of software components, we informally define a software component model by applying the same principles to all software components developed within a software process (a more formal definition of that model can be found in [54]). Such a component model provides the basis for a uniform description of software components which aids component developers and component (re-)users in properly structuring software systems and in an easy analysis of components to be re-used [57]. In more detail, applying the principle of abstraction first of all results in the breakdown of a complex software system into different types of documents like the requirements definition, the design, the code, the user manual etc. Each of the documents should be self-contained in a certain sense, ie. it should give an understandable description of the software system from a specific viewpoint. There is, however, still a lot of overlap between documents. Furthermore, there is usually no consecutive production of documents like "old" waterfall models predict, but rather documents are being produced incrementally and highly interleaved. In order to keep these overlaps observable and consistent and to allow incremental interleaved development of documents, the principle of structuring has to be applied again, ie. relations between documents of different types have to be defined and managed during software development. Each of these documents in itself is again divided into smaller pieces, because it is usually too complex to be developed by a single person as one monolithic block. Structuring such a document in itself means to apply the hierarchical construction principle and the modularisation/locality principles. Therefore the whole document is divided into a number of modular software components of the same type, like chapters of a software documentation or packages of an implementation in Ada. Again, a set of relations between the constituent software components of a document is needed, to describe how these components are assembled to get the complete document description.

These general principles can be specialised in different ways for different types of documents. If we apply eg. the essential principle of modularisation to a software documentation, it is achieved by separately numbering the pages of each chapter, avoiding references to other chapters etc. The same principle applied to a software design can be achieved eg. by dividing the whole design into a number of modules each of it encapsulating a certain data type and being independent from the context except for its interface. One possible relation between these module is the use-relation.

According to the above given ideas, a software component is always associated with a single person and therefore primarily the unit to be developed or (re-)used by a single person during a software re-use process. For the sake of re-usability the developer of a component has to provide all information which is of interest for a later (re-)user to understand the complete semantics of the component (cf. questionnaire in [7]). In addition, the component model has to provide means for integration of components of one document and even for expressing relations between components of documents of different types. In order to describe this amount of information in a structured way and in order to explicitly separate project or system specific from non-specific information we claim that a software component has to be described by a number of partial descriptions which we call views. The superimposition of these partial descriptions form then the complete description of the software component. For the illustration of the notion of views we refer to the views of the Pi-language as described in the following section.

Now, in order to describe those views in a modular way, we require, that for each view of a software component its dependency to its context is explicitly given (for a motivation see the discussion about explicit interfaces in [41]). Therefore each view is structured into three so called sections namely the export, import and body section.

- The export section describes all the services a component provides to its context.

- The import section describes all the services a software component expects to get from related software components of its context.

- The body section describes how the imported services are used to realise the exported services of the software component.

Figure 6.2 summarises this common software component model for our re-use approach, in which each document is described by a set of software components which are all structured in the same way by describing it in several views where each view is divided into an export, import and body section.

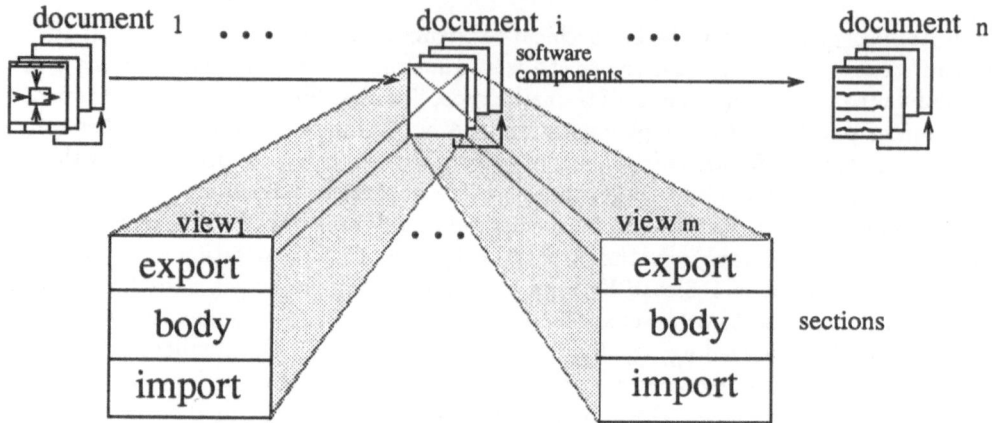

Figure 6.2: The Software Component Model

Notations.

We initially want to concentrate on the re-use of design and (source) code. We therefore selected appropriate notations for these kinds of software components first. In recent years design languages like Meld [36], the Pi-language [30], and programming languages like Ada [18] and Eiffel [41] have been developed which foster re-use. We have chosen the Pi-language and Eiffel for our further investigations. The reason for the choice of the Pi-language is — beside the non-technical historical one — its strict component model and its formal basis. We therefore have taken the Pi-language as our starting point and have already started to redesign the language with respect to re-use in order to eliminate some features of that language which complicate re-use (see [11] for more details). Eiffel has been chosen as it provides some interesting features like generic classes, assertions, and exceptions to implement specifications in the Pi-language by adhering to the above defined component model. Most of these features are also provided by other languages like Ada, Modula-2, Oberon [58] or Object-Oberon [31]. But either these languages are much more complex like Ada or do not provide one important feature as eg. genericity is missing in Modula-2 and its descendants.

As Eiffel is excellently described in [41], we can restrict ourselves to a short presentation of the most important features of the Pi-language. The Pi-language provides means for the specification of software systems which are composed of objects of specific types which communicate via (remote) procedure call. Each object is an incarnation of a parameterised object type which is specified by a single so called CEM-specification giving the data structure encapsulated in an object and the associated operations to analyze or modify this data structure. Therefore a CEM-specification is said to specify a parameterised abstract data type.

This parameterised abstract data type is specified from three different points of view, namely the type view, the imperative view and the concurrency view. In the type view the static properties of the abstract data type are specified using algebraic specifications. In the imperative view some of the dynamic properties

constructed sort Stack
operation empty : -> Stack

operation push : Stack Item -> Stack

operation pop : Stack -> Stack
  variables s : Stack; i : Item
  equations pop(push(s,i)) = s
operation top : Stack -> Item
  variables s : Stack; i : Item
  equations top(push(s,i)) = i
operation is_empty : Stack -> Bool
  variables s : Stack; i : Item
  equations
    is_empty(empty()) = yes;
    is_empty(push(s,i)) = no

type Stack **is** Sl
procedure empty **returns** Stack
  begin return sl_empty **end**
procedure push(**in** i:Item **inout** st:Stack)
  begin return sl_append(i,st) **end**
procedure pop(**inout** st:Stack)
  begin st := sl_leader(st) **end**

procedure top(**in** st:Stack)
  begin return sl_last(st) **end**

procedure is_empty(**in** st:Stack)**returns** Bool
  begin return sl_is_empty(st) **end**

path expression
  empty; (*[modifications I analysis]*)
path name list
  modifications ::= (push I pop < not_empty>),
  analysis ::= { (*{ top <not_empty> }*) + (* { is_empty } *) }

Figure 6.3: Cutout of a CEM-specification for a Parameterised Unbounded Stack

of the abstract data type are specified using pseudocode. This specification of the dynamic properties of the abstract data type is completed by the concurrency view in which the allowed (parallel) execution sequences of the operations are defined using path expressions [50]. This is illustrated by figure 6.3, a cutout from the formal specification of an unbounded stack (the informal parts of the views are optional and have been skipped here):

All these partial specifications are separated into a description of the interface and the description of the realisation of the object type. In figure 6.3 we have presented the export part of the interface of the type-view and of the concurrency view and the description of the realisation of the imperative view. In the Pi-language all object types like Stack (including the construction mechanism like Simple_list and basic types like Bool) have to be self-defined and are therefore to be imported via the import part of the interface. In order to allow an isolated CEM-specification, this import is a formal import. Therefore to obtain the specification of a system, the constituent CEM-specifications have to be connected via an interconnection language in the so called connection view of the Pi-language thus defining the incarnations of the parameterised abstract data types. This is illustrated by figure 6.4, a cutout from the connection view for an unbounded stack of character as an incarnation of the above given parameterised abstract data type Stack:

If the incarnations of the parameterised abstract data types are defined the

cem incarnation
  charstack : Stack; slist : Simple_list;
  bool : Boolean; char : Character
cem connection
  connection of charstack
    sort Sl **is actualized by** Simple_list
    operations
      sl_empty **is actualized by** empty;
      sl_append **is actualized by** append;
      sl_leader **is actualized by** leader;

sl_last **is actualized by** last
sl_is_empty **is actualized by** is_empty
sort
  Item **is actualized by** Character
sort
  Bool **is actualized by** Boolean
operations
  yes **is actualized by** true
  no **is actualized by** false
  negation **is actualized by** not

Figure 6.4: Connection View for a Stack of Characters

configuration of a software system out of objects of these types can also be described in the connection view by describing the creation, sharing, etc. of objects. For details of that view we refer to [11].

Development Methods.

The ultimate goal of a development method is to refine the general, notation independent software engineering principles which foster re-use into a set of re-use specific, notation dependent guidelines. In [2] the re-use fostering principles depicted in figure 6.1 are made more specific for different kinds of documents. This is done in a similar way in [41] concentrating on modularisation as a key principle identifying low coupling, high cohesion, explicit interfaces and information hiding as the key issues to achieve modularisation. Similarly, in [52] language independent characteristics for re-usable software components are identified. Examples for such characteristics are:

- the software component is accompanied by sufficient documentation to make it retrievable,

- the software component does not interfere with its context.

Besides those language independent guidelines, some language specific guidelines have been developed eg. for the Pi-language [20] and for Ada [28], [51], [52], [29]. The basic idea of the development guidelines for the Pi-language is the distinction between four different roles a CEM can play within the composition of a software system. The first distinguishing aspect is whether the data type encapsulated by a CEM provides a construction mechanism like the Simple_list or not like eg. the data type Complex representing complex numbers. The second distinguishing aspect is whether the data type is composed out of others like the Stack in the example or not like Boolean. For each of these roles a method is defined which guides the development of a complete type view specification, describes how to derive parts of the corresponding imperative view specification and how to derive an initial concurrency view specification from the imperative view. Starting from the already existing development method for the Pi-language and in analogy to the guidelines for Ada we intend to define guidelines for developing re-usable CEM-specifications in a first step.

Development Tools.

As Tracz argues in [55] for the tool support of some activities of the software re-use process no re-use specific technology is needed as the conventional technologies are sufficient. In view of incremental syntax-directed editors like the ones of IPSEN [24] and generators for such editors like CENTAUR [8] and PSG [1], we claim that this is especially valid for the development tools. The only new functional requirement is, that these editors have to provide support for the defined development guidelines. But this can be done by using the same techniques which are applied to check the context sensitive correctness (also known as the static semantics) of component descriptions. In that way guidelines, which can reasonably be validated during the editing process, are immediately checked and the violating parts of the component description are marked allowing an easy correction. Guidelines which can't reasonably be validated during the editing process have to be subsequently checked.

Such a development tool which is adoptable to changes of the guidelines will be realised for the redesigned version of the Pi-language within the next months in an advanced students project at the University of Dortmund [12]. This tool will based on the non-standard data base GRAS [38] which is the platform of IPSEN and on X-WINDOWS in order to allow its later integration with further tools supporting the other activities of the software re-use process.

6.2.2 Certification

In order to improve the quality of software through the re-use of software components, the re-used components obviously have to be high quality components. Therefore a lot of the work done in the area of quality metrics (see eg. [46] for a survey) is usable for determining the quality of re-usable software components. But the quality requirements for calling a software component re-usable have to be formulated stronger and they have to be controlled more strictly. In our approach some of these quality characteristics of a software component can already be assured by using the syntax-directed editor during the component development and by checking the guidelines. More complex guidelines or metrics like the degree of concurrency ([50]) have to be determined a posteriori. In addition to these not re-use specific quality metrics, in the recent time some re-use specific quality metrics have been proposed in [3]. As these metrics are neither dependent on the type of component nor on the used notation, they can be used directly within our approach.

6.2.3 Classification

A lot of different approaches have been proposed in the literature for the classification of re-usable software components. The advantages and disadvantages of these approaches and the approach we intend to realise are shortly described afterwards. For a more complete discussion we refer to [13]. A very popular classification approach is the facet approach which initially was developed by [47] and which was enhanced for the classification of re-usable software components by [44] and used by [45], [35] and [19]. Simply speaking, the main idea of that approach is to represent the whole classification schema as a set of generic terms (named facets), each consisting of a list of attributes (named terms). The advantage of this approach is the visibility and clear structure of the classification schema and its flexibility with respect to changes of the schema. That is, as the facets are independent from each other, the insertion of new facets or terms in a facet has no side effects on other facets or terms.

One disadvantage of the facet approach is the missing structuring of the entire set of components into classes or subclasses. All components are associated with a tuple defined by one term of each facet, but still remain in the entire set of components. Thus the facet approach does not allow the navigation through the classification schema.

Another drawback of the facets are the missing concepts to describe relation-links between facets, terms or components classified in the schema. Although it is possible to define a term of an existing facet as a new facet, it is not explicitly declared as a subtype relation or specialisation. The disadvantages of the facet approach are the advantages of the enumerative approach and vice versa. Simply speaking, the main idea of the enumerative approach is to represent the whole classification schema as a hierarchy of classes, where each class contains all components with the same classification. Having learned our lessons about the expressive power of the different data models as discussed in [15], and having validated the use of graphs for the structured representation of knowledge [24], a classification schema is represented in our approach as a network. But in contrast to the semantic network as described in [22] we do not only manage semantic links between components in order to express relations between components of the same type like is-used-by or components of different types like *is-implemented-by*. We additionally built up a faceted classification schema in which links between facets can be drawn eg. in order to express specialisations or generalisations. A first version of such a schema and of the associated operations for its management as well as simple retrieval facilities based on that schema are currently implemented in a diploma thesis at the University of Dortmund [49]. In a second step we intend to implement a tool which automatically determines some attributes of a component by extracting or analyzing its information content.

6.2.4 Retrieval

The retrieval activity aims at identifying the most appropriate software component in the library matching certain functional or non-functional requirements deduced from the prospective system context of the software component. In general, the approaches can be classified into retrieval using an uncontrolled or a controlled vocabulary although there are also approaches, which try to combine the use of controlled and uncontrolled vocabulary. For example in the approach of [9] a pre-defined set of category codes and some (arbitrary) keywords can be used in order to specify requirements on a component. If an uncontrolled vocabulary is used, the re-using software developer can use any significant term contained in the description of a component. For example in the information retrieval system CATALOG described in [27], every term can be used to specify the requirements on a software component, which is not contained in a so-called stop-list of nonsignificant terms like a, an, the, is. Another example for the use of uncontrolled vocabulary is the retrieval approach of [22]. In that approach a partial component specification is taken in order to express the required characteristics of a component. In contrast to that, if a controlled vocabulary is used, the re-using software developer can only use a predefined set of terms for specifying the requirements on a component. The vocabulary in these approaches is mostly given by the classification schema which is changed only in a controlled manner like the terms contained in the facets in the facet approach [45]. This controlled vocabulary is then often used to express the requirements on the software component in terms of a conventional query language for a (relational) data base system. Our retrieval approach combines some of the techniques of the above mentioned approaches: The use of uncontrolled vocabulary like in information retrieval systems as CATALOG is valuable for (parts of a) software components with a flat structured syntax and informal semantics. Therefore we want to implement that approach for such types/parts of software components like a documentation component, or the informal descriptions within a CEM-specification in the Pi-language. Using that approach the re-using software developer can get a coarse insight into the semantics of a software component.

A deeper understanding of the semantics can be achieved, if the controlled vocabulary of the classification schema is used to describe required properties of a software component. Therefore support has to be provided for the definition of a logical combination of a set of attributes. For the definition of such a logical set of attributes we plan two different mechanisms: one which is suited for novice or casual users and one which is suited for expert users. We plan a hierarchical template realised by a hierarchy of menus which represents the classification schema for novice and casual users. In a menu the user can mark alternative attributes for some criteria which shall be mapped by the required component. If we take the programming language as an example of a criteria for source code components, (s)he may mark that Pascal and Modula-2 are an acceptable programming language. For the sub-classes chosen by the criteria (s)he can then determine attributes of further criteria in sub-menus associated with those criteria in order to refine the desired properties of the component (s)he is interested in. If we continue the example, (s)he may require eg. a specific compiler for the acceptable programming languages. The user can iterate this refinement according to his/her needs until (s)he has reached the leaves. This mechanism frees the novice and casual users from knowing the whole classification schema and prevents possible errors. For an expert user we plan a query language in which (s)he can formulate a logical combination of attributes for a set of criteria (s)he is interested in directly without going along the paths in the classification schema. This query language should provide facilities like those of query languages for conventional relational data base systems eg. SQL. But the classification schema would be too fine grained if someone tries to describe the whole semantics of the software components via appropriate attributes. It is therefore necessary to specify aspects of the component's semantics which are not covered by the classification schema, by means of a partial component description. Therefore we plan an approach similar to the one proposed in [22], ie. the user can specify parts of the component in the same way as if (s)he starts to develop the component using the syntax-directed editor. Using that editor (s)he can formulate her/his desired properties by describing the respective parts of the component. This properties can refer to different views (eg. the imperative and the concurrency view of a description in the Pi-language) of the component description and to different sections (eg. the export and import section) of these views. Furthermore the properties can be logically combined by marking alternative properties, as the default for the combination of the specified properties is the and-combination.

This approach is chosen in order to provide the user similar tools for similar tasks and to assure a consistent description of the required properties through the use of the syntax-directed editor. Within our approach we implement for the retrieval by means of attributes and partial component descriptions, that the re-using software developer can choose between three different search modi. This allows three different types of matches between the required and provided properties, namely whether the required properties have to be provided at least, exactly, or partially [10]. Depending on the identified set of candidate components the user can try alternative modi and/or complete or modify the determined properties. As an example, if the search tool has identified too many candidate components, the user may determine additional properties, eliminate alternative properties, or change the search mode to at least if it was partially before and search among the so far identified candidate components. In this way the user can perform an incremental search for his/her desired component if the changed properties, or search mode do not require a search from scratch. Through this incremental search mechanism it is possible to choose exactly one candidate component which fits best with the required properties of the user. But as there are some properties of a component which can hardly be specified and measured in an objective manner (eg. readability) or for which a matching can't be completely automated (eg. matching between algebraic specifications) we intend to provide a browsing facility and report generators. These tools allow to choose the most appropriate component out of a set of candidate components through inspections and walk-throughs of the descriptions or reports about the candidate components.

6.2.5 Modification

We can not expect to build a viable library of re-usable software components without allowing to modify a retrieved re-usable software component in order to adapt it to the specific requirements of a software system. But in view of the possible loss of the components quality, modifications have to be strictly constrained and systematically performed. We therefore distinguish between modifications which are only performed by the provider of the re-usable components and those which also the client of a re-usable component is allowed to perform. The provider usually knows exactly the internals of a component and is therefore allowed to perform modifications which heavily depend on this internal semantics. As most of these modifications have to be made by hand, it is necessary to perform them systematically by keeping them locatable and adhering to the component model and the development guidelines. Therefore we intend to use the syntax-directed editor for performing the modifications. Furthermore we envisage configuration and version management facilities for managing the evolving versions as already described in [37]. In contrast to that, the clients knowledge about the software component is restricted to its external interfaces and is therefore restricted to modifications based on these interfaces. Therefore these modifications are restricted to specialisations built on top of the export interface or to changes of the components which are imported by the re-usable software component. For these modifications we do not consider any further tool support.

6.2.6 Integration

After a software component has been adopted to the specific needs of a certain system context, the adopted software component and possible further related (eg. used) components have to integrated into that system. According to our component model that means to plug components together according to their interfaces. This plug in is only valid, if in a top down approach the export interface of the adapted component matches (a part) of the import requirements of the system respectively in a bottom up approach the import interface of the adapted component matches (a part) of the provided export interface of the system. Therefore the matching mechanism which is applied during the retrieval by means of partial specifications can be used again to determine the validity of the match. The Pi-language provides by its connection view notational support for specifying the necessary renamings of sorts and operations for the -morphism between incarnations of the parameterised data types. This specification will already be supported by the syntax-directed editor for the Pi-language and a browsing tool displaying the interfaces which have to be matched. Further tool support for generating parts of that match are planned as part of the retrieval tool. Eiffel provides also a renaming clause for inherited features [41]. But as no semantics is described in the interfaces of a class in Eiffel the match is a pure syntactical one. We intend to overcome this disadvantage by considering the interfaces of the associated Pi-specifications of the classes. The problem is then to assure that a Eiffel class really implements its associated Pi-specification, which has already to be considered when associating the specification with the class via the is-implemented-by relation. Although the determination of a match between software components described in the same notation, is already a complex problem, it is not as hard as the determination of a match between software components described in different notations. We want to solve that problem — at least partially — in a constructive manner by translating a CEM-specification in the Pi-language into its associated class in Eiffel.

6.3 CONCLUSIONS

In this paper we have presented the current and future work in the area of reusability within the MERLIN-project. Due to space limitations we could only give a summary of what we have in mind on a high level of abstraction. The suitability of some of these ideas is currently validated within a Diploma Thesis and two advanced students projects. In the Diploma Thesis [49] a first implementation of a classification tool based on the classification approach presented in this report for specifications in the Pi-language will be realised on top of the non-standard database GRAS. The aim of the first advanced students project [12] is the realisation of a development tool for specifications in the Pi-language based on GRAS and X-WINDOWS. The functionality of this tool covers *an incremental syntax-directed editor for CEM-specifications which checks the context-free and the context-sensitive syntactical correctness of CEM-specifications and the observance of re-use specific development guidelines*, and an incremental syntax-directed editor which supports in the same way the specification of the connection view of the Pi-language in order to compose CEM-specifications together to software systems.

This development tool and the classification tool will be put on top of a hypertext system later on. This hypertext system will be developed within the second advanced students project [32]. The aim of this hypertext system is to allow the definition and management of relations between software components of any type or granularity and to support the retrieval of those software components according to the defined relations. These tools provide the basis for the ultimate goal of a software re-use environment which supports all the activities of the software re-use process in an integrated manner.

6.4 ACKNOWLEDGEMENTS

A lot of ideas contained in this paper came up during intensive discussions with our colleagues in the MERLIN-project, namely W. Deiters, V. Gruhn, B. Peuschel, W. Stulken, and K. J. Vagts.

References

[1] Bahlke R, Snelting G. The PSG System: From Formal Language Definitions to Interactive Programming Environments. ACM TOPLAS 1986 8; 4:547-576

[2] Balzert H. The Development of Software Systems. BI Wissenschaftsverlag Zürich, 1985 (Computer Science Series 34) in German

[3] Basili VR, Caldiera G. Reusing Existing Software. In: International Conference on Software Engineering (ICSE), Nice 1990

[4] Bayan R, Bott F, Di Maio A, Sommerville I, Wirsing M. The DRAGON project. In: ESPRIT'89; Proceedings of the 6th Annual ESPRIT Conference, Brussels, Nov. 27 - Dec. 1 1989. Kluwer Academic Publishers, Dordrecht, 1989

[5] Belz FC, Clarke LA, Osterweil L, et al. Foundations for the Arcadia Environment Architecture. In: Henderson P. (ed) Proceedings of the 3rd ACM SIGSOFT/SIGPLAN Software Engineering Symposium on Practical Software Development Environments; Boston Massachusetts, 1988. ACM Baltimore 1989 (SIGSOFT Software Engineering Notes 13; 5. SIGPLAN Notices 24; 2)

[6] Biggerstaff T, Richter C. Reusability Framework, Assessment, and Directions. IEEE Software 1987 4; 2:41-49

[7] Boldyreff C, Hall P, Zhang J. Reusability: The Practitioner Approach. Workshop on Software Reuse, SERC, Utrecht, 1989

[8] Borras P, Clement D, Despegroux Th, Incespi J, et al. CENTAUR: The System. In: Henderson P. (ed) Proceedings of the 3rd ACM SIGSOFT/SIGPLAN Software Engineering Symposium on Practical Software Development Environments; Boston Massachusetts, 1988. ACM Baltimore 1989 (SIGSOFT Software Engineering Notes 13; 5. SIGPLAN Notices 24; 2)

[9] Burton BA, Aragon RW, Bailey SA, Koehler KD, Mayes LA. The Reusable Software Library. IEEE Software 1987 4; 4:25-33

[10] Cramer J. Concurrency Checking as Component of a Software Development Environment. Diploma thesis, University of Dortmund, Department of Computer Science, 1987

[11] Cramer J, Goedicke M, Schumann H. The Redesign of the Pi-Language. Internal Report, University of Dortmund, Department of Computer Science, 1989

[12] Cramer J, Goedicke M, Schumann H. A Tool for the Development of Reusable Module Specifications; Proposal for a Students Project. University of Dortmund, Department of Computer Science, 1989

[13] Cramer J, Hünnekens H, Schäfer W, Wolf S. A Process Oriented Approach to the Reuse of Software Components. Internal Report, University of Dortmund, Department of Computer Science, 1990

[14] Choi SC, Scacchi W. Extracting and Restructuring the Design of Large Systems. IEEE Software Jan 1990; :66-73

[15] Date CJ. An Introduction to Data Base Systems, vol I & II. Addison Wesley Publishing Company, 1981 3rd edition (Addison-Wesley Systems Programming Series)

[16] Deiters W, Gruhn V, Schäfer W. Systematic Development of Generic Formal Software Process Models. Technical Report no. 29, University of Dortmund, Department of Computer Science, 1988

[17] Deiters W, Gruhn V, Schäfer W. Process Programming: A Structured Multi-Paradigm-Approach Could Be Achieved. In: 5th International Software Process Workshop. Kennebunkport Maine, 1989

[18] Department of Defense, Ada Joint Program Office. Reference Manual for the Ada Programming Language, ANSI/MIL-STD-1815A. Washington DC, Government Printing Office, 1983

[19] Dineur A, Picard P. SFINX: Tool Integration in a PCTE Based Software Factory. In: Madhavji NH, Schäfer W, Weber H. (eds) Proceedings of the 1st International Conference on System Development, Environments and Factories (SD E&F), Berlin, 1989. Pitman Publishing, London, 1990

[20] Ditt W. COSMOS — A Method for the Specification by Views. PhD thesis, University of Dortmund, Department of Computer Science, 1990

[21] Dowson M. ISTAR — An Integrated Project Support Environment. In: Henderson P. (ed) Proceedings 2nd ACM SIGSOFT/SIGPLAN Symposium on Practical Software Development Environments, Palo Alto California 1986

[22] Embley DW, Woodfield SN. A Knowledge Structure for Reusing Abstract Data Types. In: Proceedings of the 9th International Conference on Software Engineering. March 30 - April 2 1987, Monterey, California, USA. IEEE Computer Society Press, Washington, DC, USA, 1987, pp 360-368

[23] Endres A. Software Reuse: Aims, Ways and Experiences. Informatik Spektrum 1988 11; 2:85-95

[24] Engels G, Janning T, Schäfer W. A Highly Integrated Tool Set for Program Development Support. In: Proceedings ACM Sigsmall Symposium, Cannes 1988

[25] ESPRIT Project 1520. Advanced Software Engineering Environment Logistics Framework (ALF), Technical Annex, 1987

[26] Fernstrom C, Ohlsson L. The ESF-Vision of a Software Factory. In: Madhavji NH, Schäfer W, Weber H. (eds) Proceedings of the 1st International Conference on System Development, Environments and Factories (SD E&F), Berlin, 1989. Pitman Publishing, London, 1990

[27] Frakes WB, Nejmeh BA. Software Reuse Through Information Retrieval. In: Proceedings of the Twentieth Annual Hawaii International Conference on System Science. Western Periodicals Company, Honolulu, HI, USA, 1987, pp 530-535

[28] Gargaro A, Pappas TL. Reusability Issues and Ada. IEEE Software 1987 4; 4:43-51

[29] Gautier, RJ, Wallis PJL. (eds) Software REUSE with Ada. Peter Peregrinus, 1990 (IEE Computing Series 16) Extract from the book

[30] Goedicke M, Ditt W, Schippers H. The Pi-Language Reference Manual — Version 0.1. Research Report no. 295, University of Dortmund, Department of Computer Science, 1989

[31] Griesemer R, Mossenbock H, Templ J. Object Oberon, an Object-Oriented Extension of Oberon. Technical Report, ETH-Zürich, Institute for Computer Science, 1989

[32] Gruhn V, Peuschel B, Wolf S. A Software-Hypertext-System as Basis for an Integrated Software Development Environment. Proposal for a Students Project, University of Dortmund, Department of Computer Science, 1989 in German

[33] Habermann AN. Programming Environments for Reusability. In: de Ridder, ThF. (ed) Proceedings Software Engineering in the Nineties 1. SERC — Software Engineering Research Centrum, Utrecht, 1988

[34] Hünnekens H, Junkermann G, Peuschel B, Schäfer W, Vagts J. OSMOSE — A Step Towards Knowledge Based Process Modeling. In: Madhavji NH, Schäfer W, Weber H. (eds) Proceedings of the 1st International Conference on System Development, Environments and Factories (SD E&F), Berlin, 1989. Pitman Publishing, London, 1990

[35] Jones GA, Prieto-Diaz R. Breathing New Life into Old Software. GTE Journal of Science and Technology 1987; :23-31

[36] Kaiser GE, Garlan D. Melding Software Systems From Reusable Building Blocks. IEEE Software 1987 4; 4:17-24

[37] Lewerentz C, Nagl M, Westfechtel B. On Integration Mechanisms within a Graph Based Software Development Environment. In: Proceedings WG'87 Workshop on Graph Theoretic Concepts in Computer Science, LNCS. 1987

[38] Lewerentz C, Schuerr A. GRAS — a Management System for Graph-like Documents. In: Dayal U, Beeri C, Schmidt JW. (eds) Proceedings of the 3rd International Conference on Data and Knowledge Bases: Improving Usability and Responsiveness, Jerusalem. Morgan Kaufmann Publishers Inc., 1988

[39] Madhavji NH, Gruhn V, Deiters W, Schäfer W. Prism=Methodology + Process-oriented Environment International. In: International Conference on Software Engineering (ICSE), Nice 1990

[40] Matsubara T, Sasaki O, Nakajim K, Takezawa L, Yamamoto S, Tanaka T. SWB System: A Software Factory. In: Hünke, H. (ed) Software Engineering Environments, Proceedings of the Symposium in Lahnstein, North-Holland Publishing Company Ltd, 1981

[41] Meyer B. Object-oriented Software Construction. Prentice Hall, 1988

[42] Neighbors JM. The Draco Approach to Constructing Software from Reusable Components. IEEE Transactions on Software Engineering 1984 10; 5:564-573

[43] Osterweil L. Automated Support for the Enactment of Rigorously Described Software Processes. In: 4th International Software Process Workshop, Moretonhamstead, Devon UK, May 1988

[44] Prieto-Diaz R. A Software Classification Scheme. PhD thesis, Department of Information and Computer Science, University of California at Irvine, 1985

[45] Prieto-Diaz R, Freeman P. Classifying Software for Reusability. IEEE Software 1987 4; 1:6-16

[46] Project MQ; Software Quality Measurement and Evaluation. Final Report, GMD, St. Augustin & NCC, Manchester, 1984

[47] Ranganathan SR. Prolegomena to Library Classification. Asia Publishing House, Bombay India, 1967

[48] Schäfer W, Weber H. The ESF-Profile. to appear in: Handbook of Computer Aided Software Engineering, Van Nostrand, New York

[49] Schroeter U. Classification of Software Components. Diploma Thesis, University of Dortmund, Department of Computer Science, 1990 in German

[50] Seehusen S. Determination of Concurrency Properties in Modular Systems with Path Expressions. PhD thesis, University of Dortmund, Department of Computer Science, 1987 in German

[51] St.-Dennis RJ. A Guidebook for Writing Reusable Source Code in Ada. Technical Report, Honeywell Inc., 1986

[52] St.-Dennis RJ. Reusable Ada Software Guidelines. In: Proceedings of the Twentieth Annual Hawaii International Conference on System Science. Western Periodicals Company, Honolulu, HI, USA, 1987, pp 513-520

[53] The ESF Subproject ROSE: Proposal for a Subproject on Reusability. ESF Internal Document, Berlin, 1988

[54] The ESF Subproject ROSE: Deliverable A2: Definition of a Component and System Model. ESF-Deliverable, Berlin, 1989

[55] Tracz W. Software Reuse Myths. ACM SIGSOFT, Software Engineering Notes 1988 13; 1:17-21

[56] Tracz W. Software Reuse Maxims. ACM SIGSOFT, Software Engineering Notes 1988 13; 4:1-8

[57] Weber H. Software Reuse under the Software Factory Metaphor. Internal Paper, University of Dortmund, Department of Computer Science, 1989

[58] Wirth N. The Programming Language Oberon. Software Practice and Experience 1988; 18

Chapter 7

Re-usability and Software Prototyping

Ernst-Erich Doberkat
Ulrich Gutenbeil

7.1 OVERVIEW

The next section will briefly introduce the Set Theoretic Language SETL as a language for specifying programs and it will characterise SETL. Here we will indicate how Cheatham's approach [2] for re-using software may be realised using SETL. Section three will be devoted to the transformation approach which seems to be central as far as problems of re-usability within prototyping systems are concerned. Here we will first discuss dialect transformations in SETL and discuss a transformational system which translates SETL-code into Ada thus allowing re-usability of SETL-code in the production oriented environment. The fourth section will discuss re-usability in context of the so-called Hildesheim Libraries and the final section will discuss further development where we will outline a bit the development of tools furthering the use of SETL as a programming language, and we will briefly sketch an approach in which we make use of some of SETL's concepts for the pure description of software components.

7.2 APPROACHES TO PROTOTYPING

We all know that the classical model of software production using the *life cycle* approach has severe deficiencies indicating the desirability of complementing this model by other approaches. One of the more recent approaches for complementing the model is Rapid Prototyping. Having a look at the literature it seems that Rapid Prototyping is used as some umbrella notion for a multitude of activities, and it is not always too easy to find some sort of common denominator [10, 1]. We stick here to Christine Floyd's definition [9] according to which prototyping refers to the well defined phase in the production process of software in which a model is constructed which has all the essential properties of the final product, and which is taken into account when properties have to be checked, and when the further steps in the development have to be determined. We want to record for later use that a prototype is a model, and that this model taken as a program has to be executable so that at least part of the functionality of the desired end product may be demonstrated on a computer. Thus software prototypes are distinguished as models from other models in engineering: the clay model of a bridge is a model indeed but certainly no model that allows demonstrating part of the functionality of the final product.

Prototyping has been developed as an answer to deficiencies in the waterfall model, but it should not be considered as an alternative to this model. It is rather optimally useful when it complements the waterfall model. The definition by Floyd given above makes it plausible that prototyping may be used during the early phases of the design. Dearnley and Mayhew [4] suggest to augment the analytic first phase for the construction of software with the components planning and definition of requirements by a prototyping phase. It is rather evident, however, that the effectiveness of prototyping exceeds the first phase in the waterfall model considerably.

Floyd's definition shows moreover that prototyping can be used to overcome the disadvantages of the classical model. This is due to the fact that a prototype is a model and can as such be easier manipulated than a production program. It is in particular possible to proceed in an exploratory way by binding the properties to be tested to the model and then evaluate it. A model can grow so that an evolutionary way of proceeding is possible, and finally it is not required by the tentative nature of a prototype that all requirements are fixed already. These rather general statements will be substantiated by discussing some variants to prototyping.

We would like to point out here that we discuss only prototypes which are executable. This contrasts to the approach used for example in the CIP-project [3] in which specifications are used which may contain non-effective components and which are consequently not necessarily executable.

We want to develop prototyping along two orthogonal axes. One axis precises the functionality to be modeled, the second axis describes the intentions pursued by the prototype in greater detail. The functionality can be horizontal or vertical, the intentions may be classified through the categories "experimental", "evolutionary" and "throw away".

Prototypes are used for modeling functionality, consequently each prototype is based upon a set of such functionalities. Each functionality can be either of an algorithmic or of a non-algorithmic nature. Functionality which may be expressed using algorithms (sorting, managing text and data, accessing databases) are of an algorithmic nature, whereas performance criteria as throughput or storage usage, fault tolerance and ease of use cannot be expressed using algorithms and are consequently of a non-algorithmic nature.

A *vertical* prototype realises selected functionalities in each and every detail (in a way which would be done in a production program), all other functionalities are only sketched, and this is done usually only in so far as it is necessary for the proper functioning of the prototype. Vertical prototyping is apparently useful when carefully selected functions are studied in order to make statements about their behaviour. By the way, a large part of the activities attributed by folklore to prototyping, viz., constructing user interfaces falls into this category of vertical prototyping: here emphasis is laid on constructing the interface in all details while the data processing functions are usually neglected or only sketched.

A *horizontal* prototype realises all those functionalities which the final product is to realise. But this does not happen in a way which is suggested for the final version but rather as a model (so that a horizontal prototype may be composed recursively from prototypes for the individual functionalities). This kind of prototyping is most useful as an approach whenever the program to be constructed is at one's disposal, hence when principle questions regarding the entire design have to be answered.

While the characterisation as horizontal or vertical prototypes makes use of the way the diverse functionalities of the prototypes are realised, the classification in an evolutionary, experimental or throw away cares more about the way the prototype is constructed and the way it is used later on.

The bitter fate of a *throw away* prototype is characterised by its name: the purpose here is a practical demonstration of possible system functions where feasibility is emphasised so that this approach has a strong exploratory component. Prototypes which have been developed in this way are rather well suited for complementing the early phases in the life cycle model since they may be used for stabilising requirements.

While a throw away prototype emphasises exploration in order to be able to discuss desired properties and to try alternative approaches the *experimental* prototype emphasises investigating a solution with respect to its adequacy. We see here — as Floyd does — some variants in the functions satisfied by the prototypes: it may supplement the specification, refine parts of the specification (coming quite close to the vertical approach), or even mean an intermediate step from the specification to an implementation.

Evolutionary prototypes grow in different versions till they stabilise and have reached a fixed point. They may be classified according to whether they are incremental or evolving. Both classes enjoy a cyclic approach. For the construction of an incremental prototype one starts with the first incomplete solution and widens the solution stepwise to a complete one, evolving solutions are usually constructed using a cycle consisting of design, implementation, evaluation which is observed until the solution satisfies the requirement. This kind of prototyping should be used in all situations in which effects coming from the environment have to be taken into account: a prototype is brought into the working environment for the end product possibly changes this environment, and consequently forces changes in its specifications or requirements. This then requires changes in the prototype which is brought into the working environment, is evaluated and so on.

It is essential and common to all approaches that they can work only under essential cooperation of the user. Considered as a process, it is important for prototyping to seek the consensus between the developer and the user. The user is given in this way an opportunity to essentially influence the development of the final product — this is a marked contrast to the distance which may be observed between a user and the development process in the waterfall model. In prototyping the developer obtains important insights into the user's problem sphere which may soften the developer's estrangement to his product and which may allow for a custom-tailored solution. In this way prototyping generates learning effects mostly by feed-back.

7.3 RE-USABILITY AND PROTOTYPING

We would briefly like to characterise in general way the relationship between re-usability and prototyping. In order to cater for the rapidly growing demand for software it suggests itself re-using those building blocks which are assumed to be correct. It is rather difficult, however, to consider re-usability of code which has been formulated in a programming language on the level of — say — Pascal, Ada, Fortran or Assembler, since one has to take dependencies with respect to a system or upper environmental parameters. Cheatham formulates this concisely: "The problem is that programs in any concrete high level programming language are the result of a mapping from some conceptual or abstract specification of what is to be accomplished into various specific data representations and algorithms which provide an efficient means for accomplishing the task at hand" [2].

These considerations suggest considering re-usability on a high semantic level. Code may be re-used when on one hand the algorithms are laid down in a lucid way and when on the other hand not too many details with respect to the algorithms' implementation are fixed. Details which should not be fixed may be

- the detailed efficiency oriented representation of data and control structures

- environmental parameters as eg. input and output, interfaces to the operating system and to the machine

- the programming language in which the production version is to be formulated.

This makes clear that prototypes may be used as models for re-usable software. From the discussion about approaches to prototyping it is apparent that not every approach to prototyping is suitable. Those prototypes which are supposed to be thrown away are certainly not useful, the same applies to early experimental prototypes. On the other hand, an experimental or an evolutionary prototype which has stabilised may take over the desired function of a model. Since these prototypes formulate the conceptual aspects of the algorithms used in a — hopefully — concise way, it should be easy to decide whether or not in a given situation a prototype realises a desired functionality; after all cataloguing software is one of the central unsolved problems in this area. But since a prototype is not specificly bound to an environment it may be used in more than one environment.

7.4 SETL AS A LANGUAGE FOR IMPLEMENTING PROTOTYPES

SETL (Set Theoretic Language) was designed at New York University's Courant Institute of Mathematical Sciences by Jacob T. Schwartz and his group. This started early in the seventies, by the end of the seventies there have been implementations of SETL [14, 8]. The language does not enjoy wide-spread popularity and serves in particular experimental purposes. Two events demonstrated that SETL could be used for production purposes: First in April 1983 the first Ada-compiler was validated, and this compiler was written in SETL, second in the middle of 1986 an ESPRIT-project called **SED** (SETL Experimentation and Demonstrator) was launched for investigating some practical aspects of this approach.

SETL makes finite sets, finite maps and tuples/vectors available; these constructs have to be effective hence in particular they have to be finite. This is the only possibility of structuring data. The primitive data types are `integers`, `reals`, `strings`, `booleans`, and `atoms`. Apart from conventional control structures (eg. conditional statements/expressions) there are an all- and an existential quantifier which may be extended over compound objects. The language makes procedures and functions available in the usual way, programming in the large is supported by a concept of modules and libraries making separate compilation of program parts possible. The language is weakly typed hence the type of the variable is determined at run time.

It is possible with SETL to work on the formal specification of a problem. This is due to the fact that the language is particularly suitable for direct translating mathematical formalisms into executable programs in particular there are very powerful operators available which allow the user to concentrate on the essential aspects of an algorithm. Hence it is possible to achieve partly one of Cheatham's postulates: SETL is a language in which it is easy to formulate the abstract specification of what has to be achieved.

These specifications have to be complemented by possibilities of transforming the algorithm to production level. This means very concretely that these specifications have to be translated into algorithms and data structures in such a production oriented language. When referring to SETL this means that it is not enough formulating the solution to a problem in SETL for re-using the SETL-code, one rather has to have the possibility of translating programs written in SETL into code expressed in a language on a lower expressive level.

7.5   TRANSFORMATIONS FOR SETL

We have seen above that it makes only sense re-using prototypes when it is possible to transform them into production efficient versions. This is done in two steps. Since SETL is a broad spectrum language in the sense of F.L. Bauer, it is possible to program in the same language on different expressive levels:

- very close to the mathematical specification for the solution of the problem

- on the level of say Pascal or Ada so that all "higher level" constructs have vanished.

Obtaining a lower level version of a SETL program makes it easier obtaining a production version of the same program. Hence if one wants to re-use a prototype written in SETL it makes sense to first apply *dialect transformation* within SETL which has the effect that no longer any deeply nested set theoretic constructs are present. This set-less representation is then transformed by crossing a language boundary into a language like Ada. We would like to discuss briefly both kinds of transformation.

7.5.1   Finite Differencing: the RAPTS-System

One of the classical transformations in optimising compilers is reduction in strength. It rests on the observation that one may replace in loops with induction variables sometimes expensive operations like multiplication by cheaper operations like addition. The correctness of this transformation is due to the fact that invariant relations for the values of the induction variables are maintained. These observations may be extended to set theoretic constructs, for example when one has to recompute the value of such a construct after changing values of some constituent component. A typical example is the following: Let A be a set of integers, and

$$E := \{x \text{ in } A: x \text{ mod } 2 = 0\};$$

Adding a new element z to the set A one wants to compute $\{x \text{ in } A: x \text{ mod } 2 = 0\}$ for this new value of A one has the options of either recomputing the set E or —

what is cheaper — adjusting the old value of E:

```
if z mod 2 = 0 then E := E with z; end if;
```

Bob Paige [11] has generalised these observations and has developed a calculus of finite differencing for set theoretic expressions. This calculus is essentially based on identifying invariants in loops, to establish invariants and to maintain them through iterations. We would like to give an example for this: Let (V, E) be a directed graph, then the set S of nodes contains a cycle if and only if

$$\forall x \in S \cdot \exists y \in S : (x, y) \in E$$

Hence the following code tests whether or not the graph contains a cycle; the set which is printed is empty if and only if E does not contain a cycle.

```
read(E); $ E is the set of all edges
S := domain E; $ S is initially the set of all nodes
(while exists y in {x in S | E{x} * S /= {  }})
              S := S less y;
end while;
print(S);
```

Using finite differencing the more efficient but hardly more lucid code may be obtained (see [8], V.3.5.2 for a formal derivation).

```
read(E);
S := domain E;
Nachf := { }; Stapel := { };
(forall [x, y] in E)
   if x in S then
      if Nachf(y) = om then
         Nachf(y) := 1;
      else Nachf(y) := Nachf(y) + 1;
      end if ; $ inmost if
   end if;
end forall;
(forall x in S)
   if Nachf(x) = 0 then
      Stapel with := x;
   end if;
end forall;
(while Stapel /= { })
   y := arb Stapel;
   (forall x in E{y})
      if Nachf(x) = 1 then
         Stapel with := x;
      end if;
      Nachf(x) := Nachf(x) - 1;
   end forall;
   if Nachf(y) = 0 then
      Stapel less := y;
   end if;
   S less := y;
end while;
print(S);
```

(Here **om** is the undefined value in SETL, **arb Stapel** selects an arbitrary chosen element from the set `Stapel`).

Based on this calculus Paige and his group have implemented the transformational system RAPTS (*Rutgers Abstract Program Transformation System*); this system assists in dialect transformations within SETL. Quite apart from this RAPTS is able to make asymptotic estimates on the complexity of an algorithm and to make a quantitative assessment of the improvement of an algorithm by the transformation suggested.

7.5.2 From SETL to Ada

The authors have designed and implemented a system which allows translating SETL programs to Ada [6]. The basic idea for this translation system is quite easy: Take the abstract syntax tree for the SETL program and manipulate this tree till the abstract syntax tree for a functionally equivalent Ada program emerges. Although this basic idea is rather easy and quite straight forward there are a couple of principle and technical problems. We do not want to discuss these problems in detail but rather refer to [6] and an earlier paper [5].

7.6 REUSABILITY IN PRACTICE: THE HILDESHEIM LIBRARIES

The considerations above indicate what is necessary in order to make our approach to re-usability with the help of prototypes work: a transformational system for dialect transformations and a system for transformations crossing language borders. In order to be able to investigate re-usability concretely for some examples it is wise to have a basic reservoir of re-usable prototypes available. This reservoir should include important computer science algorithms.

This idea was implemented in the Hildesheim Libraries, see [13]. These libraries contain modules for many of the standard algorithms: *Sorting and Searching* is represented in diverse disguises, similarly some algorithms from computational geometry. In summary these algorithms need approximately 7000 lines of SETL-code, we have used this collection when in teaching computer science it was important to study the behaviour of algorithms or data structures using prototypes. In principle it is possible to use their Ada versions although we did not do this yet for lack of opportunity.

The Hildesheim Libraries show rather candidly one of the central problems in re-using software, viz. identifying modules. Because these modules are formulated on a very high semantic level it is rather easy to identify *what* these routines are doing and *how* they are doing it. Hence identifying components using prototypes is certainly easier than identifying components which are written in — say — FORTRAN.

7.7 FURTHER DEVELOPMENTS

7.7.1 Tools for SETL

SETL has been in doubt by its developers with a rather Spartanic programming environment, but formulating prototypes and their later use in production efficient code requires support by diverse tools. We put much effort over the last couple of years in constructing some tools for SETL in order to ease working with prototypes in this language. Let us just enumerate some of these tools. First we have built a tracer for SETL programs which allows tracing changes in values for SETL variables. This is complemented by a browser which is very useful in its support to programming in the large since it allows making dependencies of objects from each other visible and representing it on different levels. It is also possible to study dependencies of variable values form procedure calls or to have a look at the call graph for procedures over module boundaries. At present we work on a debugger which allows tracing cross references between the executing Ada-code and the corresponding SETL-code; this enables us tracing values of Ada variables back to their origin in the SETL-code. We think that this will be useful in semanticly debugging Ada programs.

7.7.2 The Tangram-System

The SETL experience has demonstrated that set theory is a very appropriate tool for describing algorithms without overloading it with implementation details. This has the rather evident advantage for the programmer that he may concentrate on the algorithmic details. This suggests using a language similar to SETL for describing algorithms on a production level. Indeed it would be desirable to blend the very high descriptive level of SETL with possibilities for program or data abstraction in a programming language. We briefly describe a program description language (called Tangram$_C$, see [7]), with the help of which we would like to support the construction of Ada programs. This has the advantage of enabling us to describe the contents of an Ada package in a suitable form on a very high expressive level when it comes to consider the question of re-usability of such a package.

The conceptual description may be done at two different points in time: first at construction time when the program is being constructed, hence when in an object oriented approach the map from objects and operations to an implementation is considered, and on the other hand at cataloguing time when it comes to catalogue the package in a software library for later use. At both times Tangram$_C$-descriptions may be used for characterising the software components. At *construction time* the Tangram$_C$-description of the package may be used as an approximation to the formal description of the algorithmic content for the package, at *cataloguing time* the process of transforming a Tangram$_C$-description in executable Ada-code which will be discussed in a moment may be reversed: given an Ada package, one is to describe this package using a Tangram$_C$-description which then can be used as specification of this package.

The connection of Tangram$_C$ to prototyping consists in using concepts of SETL for the description of Ada components. These descriptions then may be used for identifying suitable components (similarly to identifying books by abstracts, see [12]). On the other hand Tangram$_C$-descriptions may be used for generating Ada-code in a transformational way.

The language is described in [7], it is not implemented yet, and the transformational system is still in its design phase. For more information see [7].

References

[1] Budde R, Kuhlenkamp K, Mathiassen L, Züllighoven H. (Hrsg.): Approaches to Prototyping. Springer-Verlag, Berlin, 1984

[2] Cheatham TE.Jr. Reusability Through Program Transformations. IEEE Transactions Software Engineering 1984 10; 5:589-594

[3] CIP Language Group: The Munich Project CIP, vol 1, The Wide Spectrum Language CIP-L. Springer-Verlag, Berlin Heidelberg New York Tokio, 1985 (Lecture Notes in Computer Science no 183)

[4] Dearnley PA, Mayhew PJ. In Favour of System Prototypes and Their Integration into the System Development Cycle. The Computer Journal 1983 26; 1:36

[5] Doberkat EE, Dubinsky E, Schwartz JT. Reusability of Design for Complex Programs: an Experiment with the SETL Optimizer. In: Proc. IT & T Workshop on Reusability of Software, Providence, RI, 1983. pp 106-108

[6] Doberkat EE, Gutenbeil U. SETL to Ada — Tree Transformations Applied. Information and Software Technology 1987 29; :548-557

[7] Doberkat EE. Tangram$_C$ — A Program Description Language for Ada. Proceedings Seventh Annual National Conference on Ada Technology 1989, Atlantic City, 1989. pp 390-403

[8] Doberkat EE, Fox D. Software Prototyping mit SETL. Teuber-Verlag, Stuttgart, 1989

[9] Floyd Ch. A Systematic Look at Prototyping. In Budde R, Kuhlenkamp K, Mathiassen L, Züllighoven H. (Hrsg.): Approaches to Prototyping. Springer-Verlag, Berlin, 1984, 1-18

[10] Hekmatpour S, Ince DC. Rapid Software Prototyping. Oxford Surveys in Information Technology 1986; 3:37-76 (an expanded version has been published in 1988 under the title *Software Prototyping. Formal Methods and VDM* by Addison-Wesley)

[11] Paige R, Koenig S. Finite Differencing of Computable Expressions. ACM TOPLAS 1982 4; 3:402-454

[12] Prieto-Diaz R, Freeman P. Classifying Software for Reusability. IEEE Software 1987 4; 1:6-16

[13] Rüter E. Eine Bibliothek effizienzorientierter Datenstrukturen in SETL. Masters Thesis, Dept. of Computer Science, University of Hildesheim, 1987

[14] Schwartz JT, Dubinsky E, Dewar R, Schonberg E. Programming With Sets, An Introduction to SETL. Springer-Verlag, New York, 1986

Chapter 8

A Design Method to Make Re-use Happen

E.M. Dusink

8.1 INTRODUCTION

The software crisis is a well-known problem. This problem is still not solved. A lot of attempts failed to solve it, although they helped a little. Those attempts varied from tools as (V)HLL-processors to methods as programming methods and software development methods. Not all solutions proposed to solve the software crisis have yet been realised. The application of re-use, for example, is still not part of the state of the practice, although the state of the art allows it at least to a certain level.

In the Delft re-use project we will try to develop the re-use solution further. We are not so arrogant as to think to be able to solve the problem of the software crisis as history shows that as soon as possibilities increase, demands increase more. We will gain insight in the software development process at least, but we hope to solve the discrepancy between the state of the art and the state of the practice.

Re-use seems a good solution to the software crisis, especially as it is applied in a systematic way in all phases of the life cycle and within a coherent framework of: definition of re-use, method to support re-use, components to be re-used, and a support environment. We decided on component based re-use. The choice for component based re-use is discussed in [4]. A necessity for this approach is the availability of "basic" components on the application domain for which software has to be build. ("Basic" means: much used functional units.) In cases the basic components don't exist, domain analysis will result in information about the usual concepts and thus the necessary basic components.

It is also necessary to know what kind of components are available or what kind of components one wants to re-use (eg. procedure-oriented or function-oriented), how they can be re-used, how to acquire re-usable components and how to incorporate re-use in the development process before being able to apply re-use. All those things influence each other. For example if only objects (in object-oriented design sense) exist as components, a functional oriented design method will offer few possibilities for re-using existing components.

In this paper we will concentrate on the requirements for the development of a software design method oriented towards re-use. We will work within a consistent re-use framework. The framework, requirements for a development process specialised on applying re-use, and the development model itself, will be described in the next three sections.

8.2 FRAMEWORK

Re-use isn't done in a vacuum. Re-users have an idea about the kind of re-use they want to apply, a development method which supports that idea, software which can be re-used according to that idea, and an environment which supports the method.

In this case, our idea of re-use is component-based. We expect the existence of a data base with basic components of the application domain. (Basic means: much used functional units). In case the basic components don't exist, domain analysis will deliver the wanted information about the basic components.

The development method is based on the waterfall model. This choice is made because it is a model that is proven by experience. Other reasons were that most methods are based on this model and that it is the most widely known and used model.

Besides the idea about the kind of re-use and the development method, re-users have an idea about the kind of components they can/want to re-use. The software development method mentioned before has to be able to deliver (concepts of) components of that kind. In our case, we chose for object-oriented components. With object-oriented we mean the idea of packing data and operations together. This choice for object-oriented components will be discussed in the requirements for the development model.

The environment which supports the method does not exist yet. If the development method based on re-use is proved, an environment will be deducted from the tools and data which themselves are deducted from the operations described in the method. But the proving of the development method and the deduction of the environment and tools is still to be done.

8.3 REQUIREMENTS

There are several requirements for a development method based on a re-use philosophy. A first category of requirements is based on the existing framework within which re-use has to be applied. A second category is based on the fact that a working and maintainable software system has to be the result of the application of the development process. A third category of requirements is based on the fact that re-use has to be applied.

Requirements from the viewpoint that working and maintainable software has to be the result of the application of the development process are also requirements from the viewpoint that re-use has to be applied. Only the arguments for these requirements differ. The requirements will be repeated in the according paragraphs to be able to give all the arguments.

In this section we will discuss the requirements from all three the viewpoints: the framework, the development method, the application of re-use. We also give solutions for fulfilling the requirements and we will conclude with a reformulation of the problem of how to create a software development method which stimulates re-use in a systematic way.

8.3.1 Framework Requirements

In this section the framework requirements will be given. Beside the framework requirements, possible solutions to meet the requirements will be stated and a rational for the requirements will be given. We decided that a components base will exist in the environment. This components base is partly filled with at least some of the primitives of the application area.

The requirements are:

- The type of re-use has to be stated clearly. Globally speaking, two types of re-use exist. The composition approach and the transformation approach. As we discussed in [4] the composition approach is the best developed one. Therefor our method is based on components and a library filled with re-usable components.

- The development method should deliver the same kind of components as the ones stored. Thus both have to be object-oriented or procedure-oriented or whatever. The kind of the stored components has to be compatible with the kind looked for during the development process and with the kind delivered by the development method. In this way unnecessary transformations are avoided.

- The kind of the components has to be compatible with the class of languages which may be used for designing or implementing newly detected components. This improves an easy connection of components.

- The development method should deliver components on the same abstraction level(s) as the ones stored. If only architectures are stored and the development method stimulates the re-use of components on code level only, there exist a small mapping problem. With help of domain analysis, it has to be possible to get at approximately the same abstraction level(s). The level of re-use should range from architecture to binary to get the most profit out of re-use [1]. Fulfillment of the framework requirements about level of re-use is got with object-oriented development because objects exist on several abstraction levels and reflect real world entities. By this it becomes easier to apply the same strain of logic. But in this way requirements are excluded from re-use.

- The same strain of logic decision during abstraction, grouping, and interfacing should be applied for the re-usable components and the designed components. In this way an easy mapping of the designed to the stored components becomes possible. The strain of logic design is arrived at with help of domain analysis. Fulfillment of the requirement about the same strain of logic is got with object-oriented development. Because objects exist on several abstraction levels and reflect real world entities it becomes easier to apply the same strain of logic But in this way requirements are excluded from re-use. Abstraction can be done via domain analysis. Grouping can be done via high cohesion. The usage of the same logical lines also results in components which are easier to combine and easier to understand. The same development method should be used and the same result of domain analysis for the components to be re-used as for the design in which the components have to be re-used to arrive at the same logical line.

8.3.2 Requirements for a Development Method

In principle, all requirements which together lead to a good development method are a prerequisite for a development method based on a re-use philosophy. But as these requirements do not exist yet, common sense has to be used. In the following, requirements for the development process as well as the resulting products from the process are discussed. The requirements are based on the idea that the life cycle model yet to be chosen will at least consist of a design phase and an implementation phase.

While a software system is not ready at once, the development method will contain several steps. It has to be easy to understand and to follow the development method, therefor the steps have to fulfill the following requirements:

- The purpose of the steps has to be clear to be able to know what has to be done and why.

- Every step of the chosen life cycle model must serve one clearly stated purpose only to limit the concerns during development and to be able to concentrate in the best possible manner on the problems at hand. In this way the problem to be tackled becomes clear, and no effort is wasted by trying to do several things at once.

- Every next step has to diminish the potential solution space. This can be done by lowering the abstraction level, by adding constraints, by chosing from a set of solutions, and by backtracking.

- The order of the steps has to be clear as well as the relation(s) between the steps. If the relations are clear, the consequence of possible interchanges of steps becomes clear.

- How a step can be performed has to be clear. Mostly several ways to perform a step will be possible. Therefor no prescription on how to work will be given in this paper.

It has to be easy to understand and implement the design. This can be realised by:

- a design which consists of logical and abstract units. (Mind: this implies also a requirement for the stored components.) Object-oriented design is a way for getting logical and abstract units because objects are easily mapped to real world entities. Procedures are a unit of handling but not of real world entities, only if packed together with the data structures. Domain analysis can be used to get the right units.

- a design which is a loose coupling of units (less information flow). Loose coupling means that integration of the components which implements the units becomes less tedious and therefor less error prone. The fact of less information flow makes it easier to understand the design.

- domain analysis. Domain analysis should make clear the logical concepts and their relations. If the design is made with help of these concepts and relations, the units in the design will better represent real world entities and therefor they will be better understood.

- a design which units represent one concept only. This enables a better understanding of the units and therefor of the design. It also offers the opportunity to parameterise the unit with the context within which they have to work.

- clear interfaces of the units for better integration and instantiation.

8.3.3 Re-use Criteria

As the development method has to encourage re-use in a systematic way, every step in the development method should explicitly explain what level of re-use can be applied and how the information about what to re-use can be got.

Components are considered re-usable if they are logically coherent and if they are abstract. Components stored in the re-use library will therefor have these characteristics. The development method should also work with logically coherent and abstracted units to be able to re-use existing components. An object-oriented approach seems the best to get this kind of components, as real world entities are nearly by definition objects. Domain analysis can also help to form logically coherent and abstracted units.

Components are considered re-usable if they are fairly independent from their software environment. This results in, among other things, a short parameter list. A design which wants to re-use these components is, of necessity, loosely coupled.

Components are considered re-usable if they are tailorable for many applications. As far as tailoring is done via run time parameters, a design can become highly coupled. It has to be possible to get a highly coupled design. (Contradictory to the former requirement, I know.)

Components are considered re-usable if they implement one concept only (golden implementation rule). The development method should deliver required components which do so. This can be done by applying domain analysis, with which it becomes clear what the concepts are. With domain analysis, the needed possibilities for tailoring can become clear too.

It has to be possible to map units on existing components (from the components base). This enables the actual re-use. This can be done by knowing what exists during design and by adopting the same style of reasoning as during the development of the existing components with help of domain analysis. To be able to re-use components an awareness has to exist of the available components and the usual concepts of the application domain. Experienced designers/programmers use this kind of knowledge which is called domain knowledge. The importance of this domain knowledge is shown by a.o. [3]. The development method has to be domain oriented (as eg. mathematical solution methods) or should cover the process of the acquisition of domain knowledge. Another reason to be aware of existing components beforehand, is that if a design is made and afterwards one tries to fit existing components onto parts of the design, there is not much chance that this can be done without adapting the design and/or components. If design is done with the possible components in mind, less tedious adaptation work is necessary.

It is also necessary for an easy mapping that the components and the designed units have the same characteristics. Thus the designed units have to show the characteristics of re-usable components as: logically coherent, abstract, not too large a parameter list, tailorable, cover one concept only.

We chose for incorporating a method of acquisition of domain knowledge in the development process. After all, methods for acquisition of domain knowledge are less sensitive to changes in the application domain. In this way the resulting development method can easily be used in different application areas. The knowledge of which components exist will be gained by browsing through the components base.

8.3.4 Project Requirements

From our re-use project we conclude some more requirements the development method has to fulfill. These are:

- as many types of already existing components as possible should be re-usable. As most existing software is procedural and objects consists of, among other things, procedures, this is not excluded beforehand.

- units identified in the development process should be (made) re-usable themselves. As domain analysis is applied, these units should reflect concepts and thus, in principle, be re-usable. Whether or not their implementation will be re-usable depends on how well guidelines are for implementing re-usable components and how well they are followed.

Because of the requirement that it should be possible to map designed components to existing ones, the designed components already have all characteristics necessary to be re-usable themselves.

In this way, acquisition of new components is a natural and nice side effect of applying the development method.

8.3.5 Restated Problem

The problem was to design a development method which encourages re-use in a systematic way and delivers working and maintainable software systems, if applied. It is hoped that applying re-use would result in systems of better quality which would be delivered sooner then without re-use. From the requirements and the possible ways to fulfill them as described before, we conclude that the development method has to be object-oriented, domain analysis has to be done explicitly, and a components base which can be browsed has to exist.

As there exist many development methods which are proven by experience, we'll adapt an existing development method for our purposes with the requirements stated above. Which method will be chosen has to be decided on the re-use and framework requirements too, although with the requirements stated from development viewpoint an object-oriented approach is favoured.

Now the restated problem is to design an object-oriented development method in which domain analysis has to be done explicitly and which encourages components-based re-use in a systematic way.

8.4 A DEVELOPMENT METHOD

In this section a five step development method is described. For every step the purpose, the why, and the result is described. Also the re-use applied in the step is mentioned. The five steps are: domain analysis, requirements, architectural design, detailed design, and implementation and testing.

The life cycle model on which the development method is based is the waterfall model. Details for the object-oriented side are from [2].

As far as possible the requirements are fulfilled by this method. It is not possible to prove whether or not all requirements are fulfilled. The human factor remains unpredictable. Whether or not a design is easily understood does not depend on the method alone and this holds for other requirements also.

8.4.1 Domain Analysis

The purpose of this step is to get familiar with the concepts and their relations in the application domain. This step has to be performed to get a better understanding of the problem and its complexity. Also the right terminology will be mastered and the common concepts, their invariant parts and variant parts, the contexts in which these concepts work and which concepts are already realised in one (software) form or another.

The result of this step has to exist in a clear (mental) picture of concepts, their variant and invariant parts in certain contexts, and the relations between the concepts, variant and invariant parts and the contexts.

Nothing is re-used yet, but the knowledge gained will be used during all the other steps of the development method.

8.4.2 Requirements

This step has to be done in parallel with the former step. The purpose of this step is to get a clear idea of the problem (concept) to be solved and the context within which it has to be solved. This is necessary to be able to solve the right problem in the right way. The result is a requirements document. The re-use which is applied is the re-use of domain knowledge while formulating the requirements and making the decision about functional and non-functional requirements.

This step and the former one have to be done in parallel because the requirements have to be known to know on which domain domain analysis has to be done and domain analysis has to be done to get the requirements right.

8.4.3 Architectural Design

The purpose of this step is to transform the concepts mentioned in the requirements document within a certain context, which is also mentioned in the requirements document, into a contents (algorithm).

If this contents can be expressed in such a way that it can be automatically executed or transformed to be executed, the process is finished. Mostly, however, the contents is an architecture on such a high level that more information has to be provided before a new, lower level architecture can be made. If the step has to be repeated, the contents becomes the concept which has to be implemented and the added information becomes the context within which the new concept has to be implemented.

If we consider the usual way of working, the purpose of this step is to get a good architectural design which solves the problem(s) stated in the requirements document, based on a common understanding of the domain. (Good means that unnecessary concepts are omitted, terminology is consistent with the usual terminology in the domain, the architecture reflects the newest insight in the domain, the architecture is not overly complex, interconnections are kept to a minimum, the architecture is easy to understand, which means it is done in terms of the problem space and not of the solution space.)

The result of this step is an architecture of the proposed solution from which the components are, as far as economically possible, taken from a components base and the architecture itself is also taken from the components base, if possible. Or, with other words, the result is a contents of the concept which was the problem adapted to the special circumstances from the context.

Architectures as well as parts of architectures can be re-used. The validation and verification checks on this level can also be re-used. If modules of the architecture already exist they can be re-used too.

8.4.4 Detailed Design

The purpose of this step is to give the contents for those units from the architectural design which don't have contents in this phase of the development process. More context information has to be provided to be able to give contents to the concepts described in the previous result. The why, the result and what is re-used is the same as in the former step. Only the abstraction level is lower.

8.4.5 Implementation and Testing

Normally, after architecture comes design and thereafter the implementation. In terms of concepts, contexts and contents, it is a continuing story. If still the contents which resulted of former steps can not be executed or (automatically) transformed to become executable, the contents becomes the new concept to be implemented and new context information has to be added.

Purpose, reason, result and things re-used are the same as in the two former steps.

Normally it comes to implementation in a programming language. One implements the objects for which one couldn't find any components in the components base. Implementation must be done following guidelines for the making of re-usable components.

8.5 CONCLUSION AND FUTURE WORK

The requirements as described before seem sound, although possibly not complete. The way the requirements are fullfilled is open to questioning. But as long as the resulting method is not tested, we think the reasons for the solution we chose are good enough.

The main feature which makes the design method a re-use supporting method, is the repeated statement that re-use has to be applied. If this is the only difference between a "normal" design method and a re-use supporting method, we have to be disappointed about the rate of re-use at this moment in industry as well as academia. Especially so as no special tools are necessarily required for re-use.

In principle, the five steps of the development method as described before can be used for functional design as well as object-oriented design. The fact that it is intended for object-oriented design will become clear only as the how of the steps is filled in. As long as the method is described on this level, it is impossible to test whether or not the intended result is reached. A next phase in the project will be the filling in of the how and a proposal for a test of the method.

A first, very superficial, try out showed that the ideas of stating re-use explicitly and official promoting it was already a help.

References

[1] Biggerstaff TJ, Perlis AJ. Foreword on Reusability. IEEE Transactions on Software Engineering Sept 1984 10; 5:474-476

[2] Booch G. Software Engineering With Ada. Benjamin/Cummings, Menlo Park, California, 1983

[3] Levy P, Ripken K. Experience in Constructing Ada Programs from Non-Trivial Reusable Modules. In: Tafvelin S. (ed) Ada Components: Libraries and Tools. Proceedings of the Ada-Europe International Conference, Stockholm 26-28 May 1987. Cambridge University Press, U.K., 1987, pp 100-112 (Ada Companion Series)

[4] Ververs F, van Katwijk J, Dusink L. Directions in Reusing Software. Report of the Faculty of Mathematics and Informatics TR 88-58, TU Delft, The Netherlands 1988

Chapter 9

PRACTITIONER: Pragmatic Support for the Re-use of Concepts in Existing Software

Pat Hall
Cornelia Boldyreff
Jian Zhang

9.1 INTRODUCTION AND RATIONALE

Software re-use has become recognised as a vitally important method for reducing software costs and enhancing software quality. Practitioner has its own particular approach to software re-use: the re-use of concepts rather than code, working with existing software, rather than prescribing practices which will lead to the development of new software which is re-usable.

We recognise the enormous investment that is present in current software, and the very good engineering ideas that it contains, and wish to recover some of this investment when producing new systems. We further recognise that it is important to populate any library of re-usable parts (concepts), and that the richest source for these concepts is existing systems.

9.1.1 Cost of Software Production

With advances in computing technology, we are tackling problems that would have been infeasible a few years earlier. However, the cost of software increases non-linearly with size and complexity. We want to produce more software systems: how can we do it?

There are very many text books addressing software engineering, and very many companies selling software development methods and tools. Yet in spite of this there have been no significant increases in software productivity, when all ancillary activities are also taken into account. We could employ more people, but demand grows faster than our educational systems can produce suitable graduates.

We must achieve the same capability within our computer systems, but produce less code and require fewer people to do it. We could program in ever higher levels of language, moving towards specifications from which automatic programming takes over. Or we could attempt to recover the capital investment in existing software, the designs and implementations. We often produce systems similar to ones before: perhaps with new capabilities, or accommodating some technological advance, but with essentially the same system. Many seemingly small factors, like the difficulty in understanding the existing implementation or the need to move to some new language, cause us to start again.

We must be able to recover the investment in existing software: to do so is one way to break the productivity barrier. How we can do this is the focus of the Practitioner project.

Frequently the issue in software development may not be the cost of development, but the timescale: a new system must be available before some critical date, and cost may be irrelevant. This concern is closely related to the productivity concern discussed above.

9.1.2   Quality of Software Produced

The inadequate quality of software has long been a source of irritation to users of software, and a source of embarrassment to the producers of software. The newer methods, with their more disciplined approach to development, place less reliance on individual software engineers, and have made possible significant improvements in quality. But our ambitions work against this trend: we want larger more complex systems which are significantly more difficult to understand and get right.

The re-use of software concepts and components that have been in service for many years will have been proven in use. Software put together from re-usable parts will then itself be inherently more reliable. Of course the new system will contain some new software, if only the specification of the interconnections between the parts: but this new software will be comparatively small and therefore tractable.

The quality problem is associated with the productivity problem: many quality problems arise through constraints on cost and timescale, if we were more productive then we could take more care in the development of software and apply the many well-known methods for assuring quality.

9.1.3   Cost of Re-use

In discussing the above problems, it has been argued that one solution is the re-use of software concepts and components, with a particular emphasis on the recovery of investment in existing software. We have argued for benefits in productivity, timescale, quality, and personnel requirements. But all this requires some investment.

To be able to re-use software we need to identify the concepts and components that are re-usable, and describe these in a manner that helps in their re-use. We need to store these and assist engineers find the concepts of concern to them. And we need to help engineers deploy the concepts within the solution to some new development problem. All this requires investment, in the methods and tools to support re-use, and in the particular concepts that will be re-used. This investment will need to be recovered through savings associated with re-use: simple economic models suggest that very few re-uses would be sufficient.

9.1.4   The Practitioner Approach to Re-use

With its emphasis on re-using concepts realised in existing software, the project has developed and refined a working definition of such concepts, and means of their capture: a questionnaire. To guide the application and exploitation of the questionnaire, the project has developed a metamodel of re-use, investigated various forms of representation appropriate for software concepts, and initiated a programme of research applying the techniques and tools of Linguistics to the Natural Language descriptions of software concepts. Existing software has been analysed; and a prototype Re-use Support System has been developed.

9.2 RE-USE METHODOLOGY

9.2.1 The Concept

The term concept has been used more frequently in AI and in Cognitive Science [15], [4]. The way it is used there, for example as conceptual modelling, corresponds with the intentions of the Practitioner project. On the basis of that understanding, the authors have propounded the following definition [10]:

A concept is an abstract task, described by its purpose (and/or goal), the related objects, related tasks and/or the functional principles of the underlying mechanism (which will be typically, but not necessarily, of an algorithmic nature).

Examples of such concepts are (in order of increasing complexity):

- Simple arithmetic and logic operations on simple data types (one might also call these: atomic concepts)

- Stacks and their respective operations, operations on composite data types, save/restore sets of registers, synchronisation mechanisms, etc.

- Schedulers, clock-handlers, disk-drivers, buffering mechanisms, etc.

Finally, in the application domains of the Practitioner project, some rather complex concepts have been identified, such as:

- Processing of production orders in a control program, adaptive control algorithms, monitoring of material flow, etc.

This Cognitive Science view of the concept has proved to be a viable working definition. It seems to describe adequately the abstraction process that goes on in the mind of any designer, that helps a human brain to handle otherwise unmanageable masses of details. The related thought processes were first classified by Rasmussen [12] for the task of the operator of complex industrial processes, but were later extended to include the designer's task [13], [14].

9.2.2 The Questionnaire

To serve as a standard template for the capture of concepts, a questionnaire was designed [5]. This is flexible with respect to the particular detailed design descriptions used, and has been used for both textual and graphical descriptions conforming to a variety of methods.

The questionnaire requires three views of the concept:

- an application oriented view records how the concept is used (or is intended to be used) within other higher level concepts.

- a functional view specifies the input and output data, control flows, errors, and functions performed on these.

- a structural view describes the concept in terms of the composition of subconcepts, thus enabling us to capture multilayered concepts.

The similarity between the questionnaire and the IEEE Standard 1016 on Design Descriptions [2], [7] has been noted.

While the questionnaire was initially designed as a vehicle for knowledge acquisition, it has also found general use within Practitioner in other ways:

- for the documentation of new software, with the software produced within the project documented using the questionnaire.

- for software that is being captured from diverse sources, the questionnaire provides a standard format, which enables these concepts to be brought together.

- as a common vehicle for the capturing of requirements for new systems which will be built from the concepts in our library.

We are investigating how the requirements questionnaire may be matched against the library to retrieve one or more library concepts that would satisfy the requirements.

Filling in the questionnaire has required a searching analysis of what it is that is being described; when existing software is being described, the documentation and code has had to be analysed. Sometimes it has proved to be a difficult and tedious job, there have been variations in the interpretation concerning what should be included under the various headings, and there is a clear need for tools to help in this process.

In use it has been discovered that the description of versions is inadequate, and the questionnaire will need to be extended in this area. Similarly, no facility has been provided in the questionnaire for the description of generic concepts, and extension for this will also be needed. The studies reported below provide guidance in both these areas.

9.2.3   A Metamodel

Given the experience with the questionnaire, and many discussions within the project and with our reviewers, we have abstracted a metamodel of re-use [6], focusing on the data of re-use, and the process of re-use.

The data of re-use, the questionnaire, has been described with an entity-relationship model, emphasising the cross-referencing between questionnaires within a parts hierarchy. This led us to a number of simplifications and extensions, such as characterising all interaction between concepts via a single interface; generic concepts (or parameterised), with their use as parts of other concepts being instances of the concept with some or all of the parameters fixed. Initially concepts would be expected to be specific, with this genericity being abstracted later from a number of specific concepts.

The concepts captured in the questionnaire form the central data for re-use. This data is created and used within the re-use life cycle shown in figure 9.1.

In the design of new systems, the metamodel acknowledges the idea of design frameworks, high level concepts that fall between requirements and component concepts aligned with the implementation (see section 4.3 on future developments of the "PRESS").

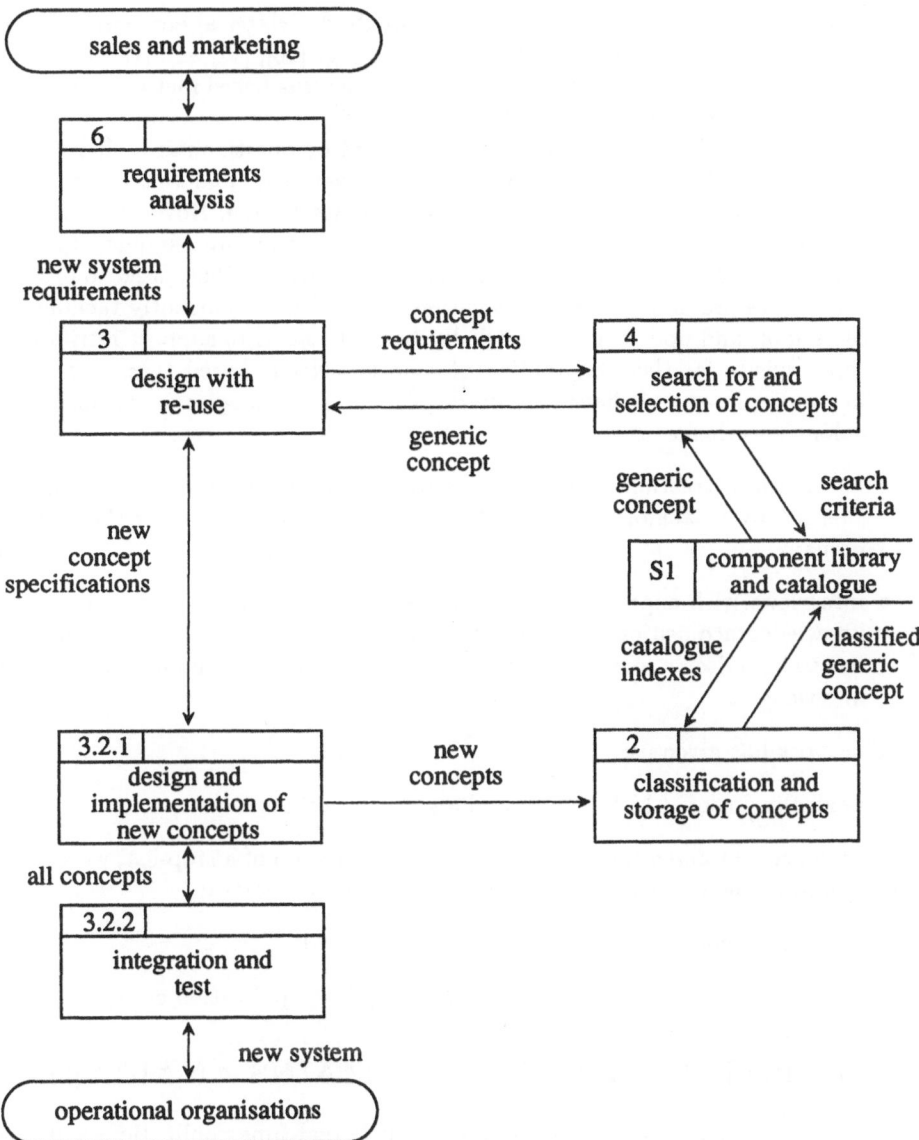

Figure 9.1 The re-use life cycle (taken from the Metamodel working paper)

9.2.4 Program Linguistics

We have turned to Natural Language Processing for inspiration in the handling of our concepts, calling this activity "Program Linguistics". Research here has focussed on:

- Classification methodology and Retrieval Strategies

- Terminology Analysis

- Classification Methods and Retrieval Strategies

We have considered various classification methods: classical enumerative, controlled index terms, faceted, and thesaurus based (eg. [16], [11] and [1]. On Practitioner we combine the faceted method with the thesaurus based method, constructing thesauri using the relevant ISO standards [8], [9].

We want to retrieve software concepts described by questionnaires. It is tempting to use the fields of the questionnaire as database keys, and this can work for some of the fields such as the name of a concept and its version. How can we retrieve concepts in questionnaires when the user cannot provide a precise query formulation? Relating terms used in a query through a thesaurus to those used to describe known concepts provides a basis for such retrieval. We are currently tackling the construction of, and updating of, knowledge based thesauri to support retrieval.

A prerequisite for the construction of such knowledge based thesaurus is terminology analysis, and we have already developed two strategies for acquisition of terminology knowledge:

- automatic extraction of index words from a natural language text, reducing this list by means of a stop word list, specifically produced for the software domain.

- interviews with experts to capture expert terminology and knowledge. Such knowledge acquisition is a quite demanding process, because the interviewer has to be quite an expert himself in order to evaluate and understand "expert knowledge".

This work has given us:

- Lexically Ordered List of Terminology, a total vocabulary.

- Frequency Ordered List, a basis for the construction of a stop list, words with a high frequency that do not support precision in retrieval.

- Stop Lists: common words and meaningless words.

- Synonyms and Alternative Terms for the various application domains.

9.3 EXISTING SOFTWARE DOMAINS ANALYSED

The project has carried out major investigations of real-time applications software, within two application domains within ABB: steel production and building automation, and within Unix. The lessons form one of these is described below.

One business unit of ABB is concerned with the design and implementation of large control systems for the steel industry. Over a period of ten years more than fifty control systems have been developed and substantial expertise exists in the department, but is mostly transferred to new projects in informal ways and existing programs are hardly ever re-used. There are usually major changes of the technological basis (hardware and system software) during the typical project duration, and several hardware families may have to be supported in parallel.

It has long been known within the department that underlying common concepts existed in the seemingly different solutions. Experiments with conventional software technology (module libraries, data dictionaries, documentation standards, software development systems) did not result in a satisfactory degree of re-use, and an analysis that this could only be solved on a higher level of abstraction, the concept level.

The questionnaire was used for the identification, description and structuring of those design concepts that appeared repetitively in the existing material. In order to be able to handle the mass of material the analysed application domain had to be narrowed down to four areas: continuous casting, strip processing, tube rolling, and section rolling.

This comprised approximately 2200 pages of documentation of requirements specification and design documentation containing both text and diagrams. It represented approximately fifty man-years of development effort. The analysis was done by one person, drawing upon other members of the department as needed. Common patterns, (ie. concepts) were described using twelve questionnaires. The work was very tedious, but yielded insights that had only been partially expected beforehand.

The main results are:

- to properly re-use detailed design concepts, a sufficiently clear idea of the overall system framework is necessary. This led to a standard structure for control software systems in steel production (see below).

- the software life cycle has to be extended by the procurement phase and the preparation of offers, which is very similar to the preliminary system design.

- terminology (and taxonomies) play a much more important role in the design and re-use process than any of the contributing engineers had expected beforehand. It was discovered that the various people involved in the design process use different terminologies and that in discussions and documents these are mostly intermixed. This results in poor comprehensibility of texts and obscuring of design ideas.

An attempt was made to separate these different terminologies in a three-dimensional scheme with axes:

- Application Axis, those terms used by engineers with expertise in steel production and overall control system design (eg. : Coil Management, Roll Program Handling, Roll Administration, Secondary Spray Cooling).

- Organisational Axis, terms for functions typically in the analyzed design descriptions, mainly used by engineers who know the organisation of production processes (eg: Order Management, Material Management, Data Table Management, System Communication).

- Data Processing Axis, terms for the implementation of DP-systems (eg: Buffer Administration, Task Communication).

At first work concentrated on the organisational axis, the most readily available expertise. It turned out that their number was relatively small and that they could be arranged in two levels of detail.

No work was invested in the data processing axis because Unix had been investigated elsewhere in the Practitioner project, and because there already existed a rich literature on data processing terminologies and taxonomies (eg. the Computing Reviews classification).

The application oriented terms became more complicated. The terms clearly belonged to the same overall category, but they could not be ordered into a structure of comparable simplicity to the organisational axis. There were narrower terms and broader terms, synonyms and semi-synonyms. Worst of all, many customers used private terminologies that have to be interpreted by the designers during offer writing.

The three dimensions corresponded with the following documentation levels:

Application Axis: Requirements Analysis, Overall System Design

Organisational Axis: Structural and Functional Specification, Overall Software Design

Data Processing Axis: Detailed Software Design, Implementation

The missing organisational layer corresponds to the phenomenon commonly observed in the use of software development methods: they only work over a limited number of levels, and then a "rupture" is observed and the method seems to be no longer applicable.

While we view this description as a little too simple, it has helped us in organising our terminology and formed the basis for our use of thesauri in our storage and retrieval system.

After several concepts on the overall software design level had been identified and provisionally described, they were combined into a generalised two-level system structure which was recommended as a basis for the preparation of offers. This was an immediate success. The engineers understood the texts of the calls for tender better and were able to detect similarities in the seemingly different customer requirements. However it was not possible to take this further, into the design of systems, and this is being researched further, looking to general theories of design, and to the use of design frameworks like those identified above.

9.4   TOOL SUPPORT — THE PRESS

Some of the initial studies involved the development of experimental tools to try out ideas — we called these pre-prototypes. The experience gained here then led us to develop a full prototype, the Practitioner Re-use Support System (PRESS). This prototype has now been completed, and will be the subject of evaluation studies. Meanwhile we are developing other tools to give us an ever expanding set of tools to support software re-use.

9.4.1   The PRESS Prototype

The metamodel of the data of re-use and the complementary model of the process of re-use (see section 2.3) have guided the specification of the prototype Practitioner Re-use Support System (PRESS). An abstract syntax has been created as the basis for tool interfaces [3]: this takes a number of concrete forms, depending upon the place of the interface within the system.

The PRESS (see figure 9.2) has been implemented by the two systems companies (CRI and PCS), with an informal data entry and manipulation system in which files

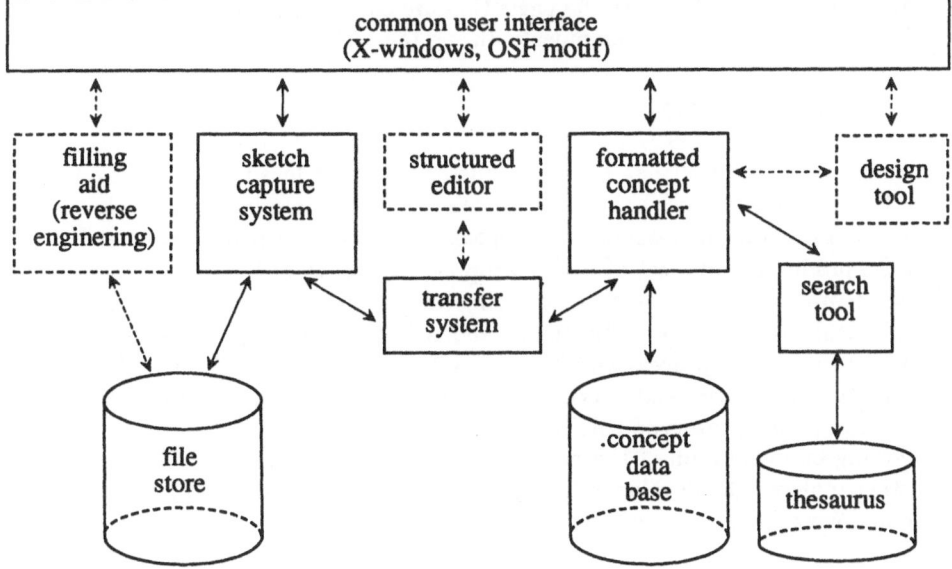

Figure 9.2 Architecture of the PRESS.

of candidate questionnaires can be entered and searched, and formal data storage and retrieval system data is stored in rigorous adherence to the abstract syntax of the questionnaire, with retrieval based on keywords guided by the use of a thesaurus. The thesaurus was developed from the domain analyses described in section 3.

9.4.2 Prototype Evaluation

This prototype will be evaluated within ABB in as near real working conditions as can be created. In this we have had to make compromises due to the limited availability of the platform on which the PRESS runs (Suns with X windows and Oracle), and the commercial sensitivity of ABB's operational software designs. While the evaluations are still being planned, it does seem likely that we will initially use the results of another ESPRIT project, Gradient, as the evaluation data.

9.4.3 Further Development of the Prototype

Developments of the prototype will be in several directions:

- basic facilities to help in questionnaire filling, such as a structured editor

- enrichment of the facilities for finding concepts, with more powerful thesauri and richer vocabularies, informed by a deeper understanding of the relationship between our thesauri and our concept base

- methods and tools to enable new systems to be designed in the context of the library of available concepts, based upon the idea of design frameworks

- methods and tools to help in the filling in of the questionnaire, from simple text search tools to help scan existing documentation and source code, to formal e=reverse engineering tools

106

Details shown in full lines are the parts that are currently present, details shown in broken lines are possible developments during the rest of the project.

9.5 CONCLUSION

The Practitioner approach has been consolidated and its feasibility firmly established. The "questionnaire" as the basis for concept description has evolved through the use of an abstract metamodel and syntax, with unifying principles that have guided the production of a set of tools to support re-use, the PRESS.

Methods from natural language processing have been used, called "program linguistics" within the project. The significance of terminologies, taxonomies, and thesauri for the design process and knowledge base has been confirmed. A broad base of material, thesauri and concepts, has been established as a sound basis for the databases of the prototype PRESS.

Following an evaluation of the prototype PRESS, improvements will be made, and further tools will be developed to support concept acquisition and reverse engineering and concept deployment during design.

ACKNOWLEDGEMENTS

The work described in this paper has been carried out with the support of the CEC under the ESPRIT project P1094. The collaborators in this project are Asea Brown Boveri AG, Computer Resources International, PCS Computer Systeme GmbH and Brunel University. In addition to the authors, individuals from all of these organisations have made contributions to the work reported here, notably Peter Elzer, Johannes Keilmann, Lene Olsen, and Jan Witt

References

[1] Albrechtson H, Boldyreff C. Software Classification: a Brief Review of Approaches. Practitioner working paper BrU-0071, 15 February 1990

[2] Barnard JH, Mertz RF, Price AL. A Recommended Practice for Describing Software Designs: IEEE Standards Project 1016. IEEE Transactions on Software Engineering 1986 12; 2:258-263

[3] Boldyreff C. The Questionnaire: a Generic Form for the Description of Software Concepts. Practitioner working paper BrU-0056, 16 June 1989

[4] Brodie ML, Mylopoulos J, Schmidt JW. (eds) On Conceptual Modelling: Perspectives from Artificial Intelligence, Databases, and Programming Languages. Springer-Verlag, New York 1984 (Topics in Information Systems)

[5] Elzer, PF. et al. Recommendations on the Use of Descriptive Methods, Practitioner P1094-WPA1.2-CRI-007, April 1987

[6] Hall PAV. A METAMODEL for Software Components and Reuse. Practitioner P1094-BrU-PH-WPB1-Working Paper, 12 January 1989

[7] IEEE Recommended Practice for Software Design Descriptions, ANSI/IEEE Std. 1016-1987, The Institute of Electrical and Electronic Engineers, Inc., 1987

[8] ISO 5964-1985, Documentation — Guidelines for establishment and development of multilingual thesauri

[9] ISO 2788-1986, Documentation — Guidelines for establishment and development of monolingual thesauri

[10] Practitioner Consortium, ESPRIT Project P1094 -PRACTITIONER: A Support System for Pragmatic Reuse of Software Concepts, Technical Annex, Version 3, 25 May 1987

[11] Prieto-Diaz R. A Software Classification Scheme. PhD thesis, Department of Information and Computer Science, University of California at Irvine, 1985

[12] Rasmussen J. Outlines of a Hybrid Model of the Process Plant Operator. In: Sheridan T, and Johansen (eds) Monitoring Behaviour and Supervisory Control. Plenum Press, 1976

[13] Rasmussen J, Goldstein LP. Decision Support in Supervisory Control. In: Johannsen G. Analysis, Design and Evaluation of Man-Machine-Systems; 2nd IFAC/IFIP/IFORS/IEA Conference, Varese, Italy, Sept 1985. Pergamon Press, 1985

[14] Rouse WB, Hunt RM. Human Problems Solving in Fault Diagnoses Tasks. In: Rouse WB. (ed) Advances in Man-Machine Systems Research, vol 1. JAI Press, Greenwich, Conn., 1984

[15] Schank RC. (ed) Conceptual Information Processing. Amsterdam, North-Holland, 1975, reprinted 1984 (Fundamental Studies in Computer Science vol 3)

[16] Tajima D, Matsubara T. Inside the Japanese Software Industry. IEEE Computer 1984 17; 3:34-43

Chapter 10

The Abuse of Re-use: Why Cognitive Aspects of Software Re-usability are Important

Neil Maiden
Alistair Sutcliffe

10.1 INTRODUCTION

Re-use of application software components faces two problems: (i) how to retrieve a software component meeting the re-user's needs, (ii) how to develop and customise that component to fit a new domain. Most relevant research focuses on the first problem, whilst component customisation has been overlooked. However, this balance simplifies a complex problem. Problems preventing successful re-use of retrieved software components are discussed, supported by results providing a theoretical and empirical basis to such claims.

10.2 COGNITIVE ASPECTS OF RE-USE

Re-using software can be as difficult as deriving or retrieving it. Development and customisation of a re-usable component is knowledge intensive, hence it is primarily a human task. However, literature discussing cognitive issues involved in software re-use has been limited to analysis of software engineer's strategies for retrieving past experiences from memory, and re-use support tools lacking theoretical or empirical foundation (eg. [2]). Studies are required to investigate effectiveness of re-use and cognitive processes which give a theoretical basis for tool support.

Successful re-use requires the software engineer to understand a re-usable component, else misuse can result in serious errors. However, investigation of program debugging tasks suggests understanding unfamiliar software can be difficult and time-consuming. Expert programmers required considerable time and mental effort to successfully debug unfamiliar programs whilst novice programmers failed to understand either the program function or structure [4]. Indeed novices tended to adopt strategies which hindered understanding [5]. Determining the effectiveness and cognitive processes which occur during software re-use is necessary to provide a theoretical and empirical basis for support tools.

Software re-use can occur at the code, design and specification levels. Whilst re-use from code libraries is well-documented design- and specification-level re-use warrant further research. Practitioner [1] and ASPIS [7] are instances of systems re-using general design concepts (cliches) which require composition, integration and customisation for a new application. However, tool support appears limited to validating component integration at the semantic level (eg. [8]). Furthermore, the common use of formal notations to represent design-level components might hinder component understanding.

10.3 SPECIFICATION-LEVEL RE-USE

Specification-level re-use is based on significant similarities between whole systems. These similarities can be based on deep knowledge, whilst surface features of two domains might be very different. Such systems can be said to be analogous. For example, an air traffic control system might be analogous to a flexible manufacturing system because their common goals require avoiding collisions between objects travelling in a space — aircraft fly along air corridors and products move along conveyor belts. Although the potential of Very-Large Software Re-use has been recognised, research has been limited to the Requirements Apprentice [9]. Advantages of specification-level re-use are three-fold. First, the perceived benefits of re-use can be felt during requirements analysis and specification, rather than design or coding, thus providing assistance earlier in the development life cycle. Secondly, re-use can take advantage of emerging CASE technologies, whose successful uptake will result in organisation-wide repositories of potentially re-usable specifications. Existing CASE environments have largely ignored the potential of specification- and design-level re-use. Thirdly, specifications ought to be more easily understood and re-used than design components, since they are represented using structured development notations (eg. Data Flow Diagrams, Entity Life Histories) intended for clarity and communication. Unlike design components, specifications describe the composition and integration of system functions, and imply the context in which design took place.

This paper discusses the effectiveness of cognitive processes observed during specification re-use. Emphasising the human role in re-use implies greater ability to customise specifications, thus increasing the potential number of re-usable specifications relevant to any new problem.

10.4 A COGNITIVE MODEL OF SPECIFICATION RE-USE

The author's work intends to support specification re-use in a CASE environment through support tools founded on cognitive theories of re-use. Specification re-use promises more benefit for novice software engineers rather than experts able to retrieve analogous solutions from past experiences. A cognitive model of re-use by novice software engineers is outlined, and implications for both design- and specification-level re-use are discussed.

Whilst no cognitive model of specification re-use exists, several investigations have suggested determinants of good analyst performance (eg. [12], [3], [10]). However, a detailed analysis of the cognitive processes and effectiveness of specification re-use was required. Re-use of abstract templates and concrete specifications were investigated to suggest the most beneficial form of specification-level re-use.

30 novice software engineers (MSc students in Business Systems Analysis, with little or no commercial analytic experience) were requested to model the JSD scheduling function of a video-hiring company. All software engineers had previous ex-

perience in the problem domain and practice with the JSD methodology. Three experimental conditions existed: ten software engineers in a control group attempting the problem without any help, ten software engineers were also given an abstract template of a scheduling function, and a further ten software engineers received the problem narrative and a re-usable specification describing a scheduling function in a production planning domain. The re-usable specification and template were both described using JSD notation. Cognitive processes were elicited by asking subjects to verbally describe any re-use as it occurred, and by questioning them once they had completed their solution — see [11] for further details.

Re-use of specifications appeared to improve the completeness of solutions produced by novice software engineers, and re-usable material presented in an abstract form appeared to enhance performance more than presentation of concrete specifications. This appeared to be because abstract templates were more easily recognised as analogous. Although both types of re-usable specifications improved completeness, they produced similar error rates; hence abstraction or re-use does not appear to help creation of more accurate specifications. Although recognition was effective, the understanding of the analogies with the re-usable specifications was not. The failure to re-use the specifications can be attributed to a lack of understanding of the analogy. Even successful re-users (eight re-used the abstract template and five re-used the concrete specification) made mistakes, many of which could be attributed to lack of detailed reasoning about the specification. Subjects appeared to exhibit a mental laziness, which, while re-using specification components, was manifested in copying rather than in reasoning. A probable explanation is that re-use offered developers a mentally easy cognitive strategy for problem solving. Similar findings were observed by [6]. A frequent mistake made by relatively inexperienced software engineers in this study was to focus on surface, lexical properties of the re-usable specification, whereas successful re-use requires recognition of deeper analogous concepts.

Findings have important implications for the design of CASE tools incorporating re-usability. Tutorial support appears necessary to encourage understanding of the re-usable specification, and to avoid analysts focusing on application-dependent surface features. Abstract concepts appear useful for initial recognition of the analogy, however, re-using concrete specifications might provide more complete solutions. Successful specification re-use can benefit novice analysts in three ways: first, they are an important source of domain knowledge deprived from novice analysts by their lack of experience. Secondly, it can assist in structuring the analyst's problem-solving strategy, and suggest the scope of the new system. Thirdly, solution testing is a determinant of good analytic performance: re-usable specification can provoke evaluation of new specifications by providing alternative scenarios in which to test them.

Results have implications for code- and design-level re-use. First, understanding complex code fragments is an odorous task, hence mental laziness may be even more likely when re-using design- or code-level components. Secondly, many researchers emphasise automated software re-use, however, the complexity of their tasks is put into perspective when we consider the difficulties encountered by intelligent software engineers. Successful automated re-use might only be achievable by tools with knowledge bases and reasoning capabilities beyond the scope of today's systems. Increased productivity and quality may better be achieved by a more pragmatic approach which recognises the strengths and limitations of both tools and human re-users. Recognising the need for human involvement seems inevitable if we are to exploit the rich seam of software repositories currently available to software developers.

References

[1] Boldyreff C. Reuse, Software Concepts, Descriptive Methods and the Practitioner Project. ACM SIGSOFT Software Engineering Notes, 1989 14; 2:25-31

[2] Fischer G. Cognitive View of Reuse and Redesign. IEEE Software, 1987 4; 4:60-72

[3] Guindon R, Curtis B. Control of Cognitive Processes During Software Design: What Tools are Needed? In: Soloway E, Frye D, Sheppard SB. (eds) CHI'88 Conference Proceedings; Human Factors in Computing Systems; May 15-19 1988 Washington DC. Addison-Wesley, Reading 1988 pp 263-269

[4] Holt RW, Boehm-Davis DA, Shultz AC. Mental Representations of Programs for Student and Professional Programmers. In: Olsen GM, Sheppard S, Soloway E. (eds) Empirical Studies of Programmers, Second Workshop. Ablex, Norwood NJ, 1987 pp 33-46

[5] Nanja M, Cook RC. An Analysis of the Online Debugging Process. In: Olsen GM, Sheppard S, Soloway E. (eds) Empirical Studies of Programmers, Second Workshop. Ablex, Norwood NJ, 1987 pp 172-184

[6] Novick LR. Analogical Transfer, Problem Similarity and Expertise. Journal of Experimental Psychology: Learning, Memory and Cognition 1988 8; 5:484-494

[7] Puncello PP, Torrigiani P, Pietri F, Burion R, Cardile B, Conti M. ASPIS: A Knowledge-Based CASE Environment. IEEE Software 1988; :62-72

[8] Rice J, Schwetman H. Interface Issues in a Software Parts Technology. In: Biggerstaff TJ, Perlis AJ, (eds) Software Reusability: Concepts and Models. ACM Press, 1989

[9] Rich C, Waters RC, Reubenstein HB. Towards a Requirements Apprentice. MIT Artificial Intelligence Laboratory, 1987

[10] Sutcliffe AG, Maiden NAM. Analysing the Analyst: Investigation of Cognitive Models in Software Engineering, submitted for publication, 1989

[11] Sutcliffe AG, Maiden NAM. Software Reusability: Delivering Productivity Gains or Short Cuts? To appear in proceedings SE-90, Brighton UK, 1990

[12] Vitalari NP, Dickson GW. Problem Solving for Effective Systems Analysis: An Experimental Exploration. Communications of the ACM 1983 26; 11:948-956

Chapter 11

Design-Aspects supporting Software Re-use

Roland Mittermeir

11.1 DESIGN FOR RE-USE — GENERIC DESIGNS

There seems to be a marked difference between software design and data base design. The software designer solves the task having a particular application in mind, whereas the data base designer solves the task having a particular subsection of the (his !) "world" in mind. This distinction might seem hypocritical — however, it surfaces as soon as one starts thinking about Object-Oriented Design [2].

11.1.1 Generic Designs

One of the major claims put forward by some advocates of object-orientedness is that a special design effort is superfluous, since object-oriented software is a one-to-one image of real world entities (objects), combining their states and their capabilities (instance variables and methods), falters, as soon as one strives for optimising a design and as soon as one addresses systems having a strong (may be object-oriented) action-bound aspect as well as a strong (may be object-oriented) data-bound aspect. Taking care of both aspects requires conceptual modelling and in doing so, one immediately reaches the problem that one needs to talk about model classes and model instances. The distinction into model classes and model instances — and hence the need for generic designs when adhering to an object-oriented design discipline — becomes apparent at least at the following occasions:

- when extending the model boundaries by integrating a new object will have more than local effects on the overall model (on some instances of the overall model!);

- when a more refined specialisation of some object (one, which has not been considered necessary at the outset) leads to corresponding refinements in other objects;

- when considering non-trivial relationships between objects requires to place integrity constraints over object- and/or message-structures [4].

The integrity constraints mentioned above cannot (should not) be part of the individual objects, since they are absolutely application dependent. In classical software- or data-engineering, such integrity constraints would be taken care of by application programs, ascertaining their preservation on modifications of the data base. In object-oriented programming, they would either be taken care of by some of the concerned objects (thus leading to non-symmetric or rather complex solutions, which are not very nice indeed), or by an object manager to be invoked when peeling a particular application out of some object-oriented design.

While object-oriented design has the potential of integrating knowledge from data base design with knowledge from software design, the above arguments show that there is far more to it than simply merging the two disciplines. We are convinced that there is still much work to be done on this issue and we plan to investigate it further in the next future.

11.1.2   Steps in Object-Oriented Design

An issue we feel more confident about, is the question as to what needs to be specified in a first-cut object-oriented design and what the basic steps might be in such a methodology [5]. Building on the axiom that designing according to the object-oriented paradigm will lead on the conceptual level to generic — and hence re-usable — designs, we have to classify object-oriented systems as systems consisting of interacting processes. Thus, we consider the approach proposed in [1] for specifying processes as least constraining while allowing already various levels of cross-referencing and cross checking.

To sketch this briefly, we conceive of a (generic) system as a system consisting of some (still rather general and high level) objects interacting in a very general way. Taking this viewpoint versus the subsection of reality to be modelled, we propose the following sequence of steps:

1. identify those "most abstract" objects

2. identify their (obvious and "abstract") interactions

3. object specification

4. object integration

5. normalisation

6. refinement

Step 1.) seems obvious. It is important to note though that here we do not yet do any refinement on those objects. We could think of it rather as a kind of brainstorming, searching what is there and, after this has been done, leaving aside for the moment anything which is already too implementation dependent or which is to be considered an artefact of the particular application(s) one has in mind when doing this exercise.

Step 2.) serves as a kind of cross-validation for step 1.). If objects identified are in no relationship whatsoever to the rest of the system, then probably they either do not belong to it or something has been forgotten in the specification.

Steps 1.) and 2.) focus on the overall system. With the information they yield, we may in step 3.) specify each individual object in a precise formal manner. Doing so, we firstly identify the domain of messages an object accepts, and the domain of messages it provides. By means of axioms, the input/output behaviour is given, and simplification rules will essentially define invariances over the input stream of the object (and hence essentially provide the information an implementor might need to define the states and their structure [data structure] of the object).

In step 4.), object integration, one checks whether the messages received by any object are specified to be sent by an object and whether those sent are received somewhere. Having successfully completed this object integration step, one can feel ascertained that one has an internally consistent model at hand. As a kind of weak completeness check, one can examine whether the message structure resulting from step 4.) completely represents the loosely defined interactions identified in step 2.).

Next, step 5.), one has to check whether this model is sound (see next section on normalisation), and if not, split the objects identified so far into normalised ones. Having thus a sound model at a given level of refinement, one may progress to the next step.

With object refinement (step 6.), our task is inherently identical to the task pattern outlined in steps 1.) and 2.). Hence, our methodology is recursive in the steps outlined so far. The general refinement differs from initial object- and message-identification only in so far as it is extended by a (strict) verification sub-step, checking that each message on the previous level of refinement has a corresponding (set of) lower level message(s).

11.2   NORMALISATION CRITERIA FOR SOFTWARE

With software normalisation [6], [7] we are referring to a design step, which, similarly to database normalisation, will make a design "update-able" and "re-combinable", hence: re-usable.

The key idea allowing to define criteria for normalising software on a semantical level was found in the work on relational program specification [3]. There, a piece of software is specified by considering its analogue in the form of a relation, being a subset of the cross product of domain and range of the program-function.

With this static description, functional dependencies could be defined. They gave rise to normalisation criteria similar — but not identical — to those in data base design.

For various reasons — complexity and the later composition of software out of normalised components (see also the companion paper [8]) being important aspects in this decision — normalisation criteria have been defined distinctly for memoryless functions and for state bearing objects [7]. Informally, these normalisation rules could be described as follows:

Normalisation of functions

FN1: A design unit is **fully transient**, iff it is free from side effects and the input arguments have the key property.

FN2: A fully transient design unit is **irreducible**, iff it can be expressed in closed form. (ie. if it is not semantically meaningful to horizontally partition the program relation).

FN3: A fully transient design unit is **elementary**, iff there are no functional dependencies between any proper subsets of its flattened arguments.

FN4: An irreducible elementary design unit is **atomic**, iff no semantically complete proper subset can be defined over the set of output arguments.

Normalisation of processes:

PN1: A process p(X; Y) is **transparently specified**, iff under consideration if its state space S, its process function [[p]] = f(X, S; Y S') satisfies FN1 (is fully transient).

PN2: A transparently specified process p(X; Y) is **irreducible**, iff its state space cannot be partitioned in such a way that there exists not at least some connection between its instances via the related program function f.

PN3: A transparently specified process p(X; Y) is **elementary**, iff the process function [[p]] = f(X, S; Y, S') with S being unfolded, satisfies FN3. (A state space is unfolded, if it does not contain an attribute with a domain being the encoding of some folding of otherwise independent attributes.)

PN4: An irreducible elementary process p(X; Y) is **atomic**, iff there is neither a semantically complete proper subset over its output attributes nor over attributes over its unfolded state space.

11.3   SUMMARY

This paper sketches the methodological work we are doing in Klagenfurt to support design for re-use and object-oriented design. This work builds on the premises that object-oriented design shares several important aspects with data base design. One of the markedly common aspects is that we propose a distinction between conceptual modelling and physical modelling. The two phases have different goals, the detailed steps show structural similarity though.

Building on the notion of conceptual modelling, a normalisation procedure for software components has been proposed. This procedure has been originally defined just with the aim of re-use in mind. It can be extended to object-oriented modelling a rather straight forward manner.

References

[1] Boudriga N, Jaoua A, Mili A, Mittermeir R. A Generalized Model for Program Specifications. Department of Computer Science, University Tunis, Tunis, 1988

[2] Forschungswoche Informatik, Pörtschach, 1989

[3] Mili A, Desharnais J, Mili F. Relational Heuristics for the Design of Deterministic Programs. Acta Informatica 1987 24; 3:239-276

[4] Mili H, Sibert J, Intrator Y. Relationships as Semantic Constructs in Object-Oriented Programming. In: Proceedings 10th Tunesian-French Seminar of Computer Science, Tunis, 1989

[5] Mittermeir RT. Object-Oriented Software Design. In: International Workshop on Software Engineering Environments, Beijing China, 1986

[6] Mittermeir RT. A Normalization Theory for Software Components. In: Proceedings of the 1-ier Séminaire Internationale sur le Génie Logiciel á Oran, Oran Algerie, 1988

[7] Mittermeir RT. Normalization of Software to Enhance its Potential for Reuse. TR UBWI 6/89, 1989

[8] Rossak W, Mittermeir RT, Hochmüller E. Structures for Supporting Software Reuse. In: Dusink EM, Hall PAV (eds) Software Reuse: the European Approach. Springer, 1991

Chapter 12

Structures for supporting Software Re-use

W. Rossak
R.T. Mittermeir
E. Hochmüller

12.1 THE SOFTWARE ARCHIVE

12.1.1 Basic Considerations

The concept of the Software Archive [9] is based on the idea to improve the production of conventional (business oriented) software systems by means of re-use of existing software — so called components — stored in a kind of specially structured library.

There is no restriction concerning the level of refinement or the comprehensiveness of the contents administered within a Software Archive. Neither are there any restrictions regarding the level of representation of a component referred to imposed by the Archive. Likewise, one is free with regard to the method or technique used during the development process. This means that there is no special analysis or design method which favours or inhibits the use of a Software Archive and there is no restriction concerning the programming language used in the implementation phase. (However, we think that an adapted top-down approach or a prototype based approach would allow to benefit best from the components represented in a Software Archive [10].)

Hence, the Software Archive is a repository of possibly re-usable components in its most general form, supporting "development with re-use" by indexing, classifying, describing and supplying the products necessary in a software development project.

This relatively pragmatic basic concept is completed by the following goals:

- Support for software re-use must be project independent.

- A search process in the Software Archive must be user oriented.

- The tool which implements the Software Archive must be based on technologies available in the software industry.

The goal of project independence strives to overcome the necessity to search the structures of old systems to find a fitting re-usable component. Possibly re-usable components must be stored in a structure of their own, making classification and search independent from the necessities of the project they were originally developed for. Thus, the structure of a Software Archive allows to generate a kind of catalogue of existing components, which can be adapted to the different points of view of different user groups. Section 1.2 gives a short introduction to this structure.

The search process in the Archive is based on this structure and allows the user to retrieve software components in a step by step fashion. While browsing through the archive, the user enriches the initial search specification, while zooming in on potential candidates for plain re-use or for adaptation. Adding details as late as possible, while making decisions between similarly fitting components, leads to a search-pattern which is similar to the "shopping paradigm". This is opposed to search algorithms which force the developer to define the component searched for in full detail in advance (section 1.3).

A tool which implements the Software Archive must be able to handle the needs given in a development environment which is oriented towards business applications. Furthermore, it must be usable without major investments in new technologies and concepts, not commonly available at the currently given state of development in industry. Therefore, the prototype implementation of the Software Archive, the Archive Manager, is based on a standard relational DBMS. The major features of this Archive Manager are presented in section 1.4.

12.1.2   The Structure of the Software Archive

The Software Archive realises the above mentioned concepts and goals in two ways [8]:

- The units of re-use, the components of the Archive, are modules derived during a conventional development process.

- These components are embedded in a structure, which allows to support project independent classification and development, while being flexible enough to reflect different points of view of different users.

A component in the Software Archive is simply a module which had been developed in a former project and which was classified and incorporated in the Archive. It is not bound to a certain level of decomposition, to a certain kind of representation or to a certain stage of development. It can thus be a specification of a whole software system or merely the source code of a test-procedure. Its description consists (simplified) of three parts:

- a component type,

- a contents definition,

- interface and placement/positioning information.

The component type gives a very rough first classification of each component in the Software Archive, independent from its position in the search structure and from its relations to other components. A component may be classified as:

- a function,

- a data-structure or

- a system resource.

A component is classified as function or data-structure according to its major use on the given level of abstraction/development. However, it is classified as a system resource if it is outside the scope of the development project and is used just as a given prerequisite which supports the development process (eg. a database system).

The contents definition includes the description of the component (or a reference to it) which was derived during the original development process. This description is the core of the component's contents definition and determines all the other items describing the component and its place within the structure of the Software Archive. The description is in the form and notation which had been used in the respective project.

However, there are considerations to find a kind of standardised formal component description, which would allow to abstract from the project dependent level of representation used so far [1]. These considerations lead also to the proposition of semantic normal forms for components. These concerns of "development for re-use" are dealt with in [7].

The other major part of the content definition of a component are attributes, which are derived from the description. They are standardised in their form of representation and with respect to used types and metrics. They describe the component in a more standardised way and distinguish it from similar ones in the Archive's structure. These attributes are inherited in the generalisation hierarchy of the Software Archive (see below).

The interface and placement information serves to document the relations to other components in the Software Archive. These relations form the structure of the Archive which is based primarily on two classification/search dimensions:

- Decomposition/Aggregation.

- Specialisation/Generalisation.

The decomposition dimension, implemented by PART-OF relations, allows to build an aggregation hierarchy, similar to those used in system development. However, the PART-OF relation used in the Software Archive does not ensure any completeness of decomposition of a superordinate component nor does it prevent duplicate decompositions, ie. the modeling of possible alternative subordinate components. Furthermore, the idea is not to describe the structure of a full application system. The only function of this dimension is to allow a classification based on the well known decomposition/aggregation concept for modules.

Specialisation/Generalisation is expressed by IS-A-relations between components on one level of decomposition. It is used to document the similarity between stored components and to organise the inheritance of common attributes in the component description from superordinate to subordinate components. This dimension implements the basic idea to organise the Software Archive in such a way that classification and search-processes are adapted to the way of human thinking and to the work in a development group: Modules on different levels of generalisation are grouped in a classification schema, leading from very general components, related to early phases of development, to very specialised ones, describing modules on source-code level.

Since similarity is a semantic concept, different user groups of the Archive have the possibility to define different generalisation hierarchies, reflecting different points of view of classification by similarity. These different views of classification, so called "user views", correspond to alternate search environments which are adapted to the needs of different development projects using the Software Archive.

12.1.3 Searching in the Software Archive

A search in the Software Archive can be conducted in each phase of system development, thus supporting the idea of a "development with re-use". The goal of such a search process is to identify possible re-usable components which can be used as prefabricated "building blocks" [10]. (Note, however, that the stored components are products of a conventional development process and not products of a "design for re-use" approach — cf. [2, 3] and [7].) This will be advantageous, provided that an already existing component of the Software Archive will need less further development and test effort than a component which has to be produced from scratch.

The input for a search process is the specification of the needed system-component which has been derived by a developer at the current stage of system development. This target specification should be on the highest possible level of abstraction and contain no unnecessary details ([9], [10]). This target specification is compared to the component definitions stored in the Software Archive. Details are added to the target specification in a step by step fashion while browsing through the supply of components given by the Software Archive.

This leads to a search which is guided on one hand by the target specification, which defines the "hard", not alterable preconditions, and on the other hand by the structure of the Software Archive, which allows to check the different possible solutions stored in the repository. These solutions may differ in the details they add to the target specification and/or in the way they implement the specified abstract concepts on the next level of realisation.

We call this approach the "shopping paradigm". The idea is the same as with shopping in a supermarket: I try to get what I want by adapting my needs as far as possible to the given supply. To be able to do so, I have to "specify" my needs in a way which is general enough to allow me to abstract from details and to evaluate alternatives. However, I will ensure that only valid "solutions" are considered. Hence, if no satisfying solution is on hand, I will buy the product I am looking for somewhere else.

From a more technical point of view, a search process in the Software Archive is oriented on the structure given by the relations describing the decomposition and generalisation/similarity dimension [6]:

It starts at a level of decomposition which is derived from the needs of the current stage of development. At this level of decomposition the developer determines the user view which provides the best structuring concept for his needs. Within a user view, a highly generalised component, which fits the target specification, is selected. This "generalisation class" is the root of a tree shaped structure of similar re-usable components. These components differ from each other with respect to alternative solutions for given concepts and/or with respect to added details.

By adding details and making choices between available specialised alternatives, the search process continues. If no component can be identified as being a possible candidate for re-use, the original level of decomposition, the current user view or the chosen generalisation class can be varied.

Finally, either a fitting component is found, or a similar one, which needs some modifications, is marked. If no component of the Software Archive seems to be a candidate promising enough for re-use, the component can be developed from scratch or on the basis of one of the intermediate component descriptions which have been the best approximation to the target specification without being a match. In all cases of component development the new component will be classified and stored in the Software Archive for later use.

12.1.4 The Archive Manager Prototype

The concepts of the Software Archive, as described above, have been implemented on the basis of a relational DBMS as a first prototype, the Archive Manager [11]. The reasons for choosing a standard relational DBMS instead of an object oriented one and to use none of the sophisticated AI tools available on the market, which would have supported the implementation of the different relations in a Software Archive in a more sophisticated way, are discussed in [9] and in [11]. However, there are two main ideas which lead to this decision:

- The Archive Manager must be able to administer a lot of data (components).

- The Archive Manager should be based on currently available technology.

To be able to support software re-use in the way described above, it is necessary to store components from a lot of different projects and from different phases in these projects. This means that an Archive Manager will have to hold and to administer an amount of data which is typical for DBMS systems and cannot be managed by the AI tools which are available at the current state of the art. Furthermore, an Archive Manager will have to support a multi-user environment and ensure strict data consistency, concepts which are not common in most AI tools.

Besides these conceptual problems, it is attractive for the software industry to be able to work in a stable and tested environment based on a technology which is well known and reliable. A DBMS based tool can provide all these features in the best way. The use of a relational DBMS instead of an object oriented one will guarantee that the necessary system resources are available not only in labs but also in each software house at the current stage of industrial tool usage.

A prototype of the Archive Manager has been developed with about fifteen tables modeling the basic structure of a Software Archive and some more tables to support administrative necessities. He supports a menu-driven user-interface for alpha-numerical terminals and supports three different user-classes:

- the normal user/developer,

- the privileged user,

- the Archive Manager administrator.

The system is divided into two main parts

- component handling and

- internal handling.

"Component handling" is used by privileged and normal users, "internal handling" is reserved for the administrator.

A normal user is a developer who is working in a project group. He may search in the Software Archive and retrieve components and their descriptions. The Archive manager supports him by giving him choices and menus to determine the necessary level of aggregation and the user view he wants to work with. Within a user view the system leads him through the similarity structure of the view in a kind of manually controlled back-tracking algorithm.

A privileged user is related to a certain development project and is the technical specialist for the Archive Manager in this group. He is not only allowed to search into the Archive, but can also insert (classify) and delete components.

At start-up time of an Archive Manager system, the Archive Manager administrator can tune some standards and consistency rules, overwriting the defaults of the underlying Software Archive. Doing so, he is able to adapt the basic structure of the Software Archive to the needs of the company and the typical phases of the development process in use. During run-time, he supports the privileged users and ensures the defined standards. Furthermore, he has utilities which enable him to handle the necessary administrative functions, like user-id handling, consistency checks and weekly statistics.

The current stage of development of the Archive Manager is that of a prototype which has been implemented and tested by students. We are looking forward to test and to verify the Archive Manager tool and the concepts of the Software Archive in an industrial environment.

12.2 THE SOFTWARE BASE

12.2.1 Basic Considerations

In contrast to the Software Archive, the Software Base supports re-use on the code level [4], [5]. The basic idea behind the concept of a Software Base is strongly connected with the desire to hand over parts of the software development process to the end-user in order to reduce the software development backlog. Since end-users are supposed to be only moderately trained "programmers", the software base needs to support a very safe and sugar-coated development process. As an analogue paradigm, we used end-user facilities of data base management systems. Similarly to working with a DBMS, a "query" against a Software Base will yield candidate-programs which may be composed without injecting too much external knowledge. This will work much along the lines as joins will compose new tuples out of sets of joinable tuples from data base relations.

In the database field, a database administrator is responsible for providing an adequate conceptual data model, for defining appropriate integrity constraints, and for maintaining particular views for the various users of the data base. In the Software Base Management System the contents to be "managed" are programs which can be composed according to a set of stratified integrity constraints in order to get a new or modified software system. In analogy to the database example, a Software Base Management System is provided.

12.2.2 Principles of Software Bases

Programs constituting a software system can be classified according to the application in which they are used and according to the function or task they perform. Similar applications can be organised in a common application category, whereas similar tasks can be grouped into task categories. In order to allow successful re-use, one of the following three conditions should hold for programs within a particular task category:

- programs used for different applications are identical,

- programs with differences on the code level can be substituted for each other,

- programs of the task category are similar in such a way that there exists some common code which can be considered to be a generalisation of all the programs of that task category.

The concept of the Software Base dwells on the third case. Thus, each task category has its specific so-called program generic which is a program skeleton describing the invariant properties of the particular task category. Furthermore, for each task category, there exists a set of specialisation rules guiding the refinement concerning interfaces on program level, algorithmic structure as well as data encapsulated by the program. The individual procedures or programs, constituting the original instances from which the task category has been derived, may then be regained by detailing data definitions, algorithmic portions and interface structures left open in the generic. New variants of a task will be generated by refining the specialisation rules defined for each task category.

Since a company will usually have several classes of moderately similar applications, the notion of genericity and refinement is replicated on the application level. Hence, the Software Base provides for a generic application framework for each application category, the application lattice, which is — in analogy to the program generic — a generic structure for all applications of a particular class. This structure can be refined on the control level as well as it may have constraints regarding program usage. Linking the refined programs into this structure will yield a particular instance of an application.

12.2.3 Software Base Management System

To support prototyping and to allow the placing of such a tool into the hands of only moderately trained users, a neat Software Base Management System (SBMS) must be provided which supports the refinement process of getting executable programs out of program generics as well as the composition of those programs yielding a new application system constructed by end-users. The flexibility of these processes is bounded by a two-level-structure of integrity constraints referring to integrity levels within the refinement of programs as well as to integrity constraints concerning the refinement across tasks. They are expressed in so-called program interface matrices and task interface matrices.

Further, there are precautions for integrity preservation across the whole system. These are supported by a role model, where — in analogy to DBMS's — a software base administrator (SBA) will be responsible for integrating task- (and application-)

categories into the SBMS. The SBA defines for each task category-type the program generic and the associated specialisation rules concerning data and algorithmic parts as well as the task interface definition. Regarding the application system the SBA provides the application generic — the so-called application lattice which provides the skeleton code to integrate tasks into a full application — together with the associated composition rules. In doing so, built-in integrity constraints have to be obeyed. Additionally, the software base administrator defines constraints which must be obeyed by the other people involved in the system building process.

According to given constraints and specialisation rules, the programmer integrates the program generic jointly with his specialisations on data and algorithm to an executable program. He may on his part specify constraints concerning the integration of the refined programs into an application.

Finally the application composer constructs a new application by integrating the task-level programs into the application lattice. He has to observe composition constraints and may specify on his turn usage constraints [5].

In organising all programs of an application category in a matrix where the row label indicates the name of the application they serve, and the column label is represented by the name of the task being performed within the application, the database analogy is clearly seen in the process of application composition by considering the individual task categories the attributes and regarding the individual names of applications as keys of application tuples with programs representing their attribute values.

A first prototype providing a SBMS according to the above concepts is in the design stage. The system will support four different user-classes in sustaining their particular roles:

- the software base administrator who defines the program generics and associated specialisation rules as well as the application lattice and connected composition rules,

- the expert programmer who refines the given program generics with specialisations written in a conventional high level language to get executable programs,

- the application expert who builds his own application by combining the programs already provided within the given framework,

- the application user whose work is supported by the various applications.

The prototype will be realised under a UNIX operating system using Ada as implementation language. The main reason for choosing this development environment stems from the desire of using a powerful operating system and a language with supports interfaces to other programming languages. This is important in order to provide support for programs stored in the software base which would not necessarily be written in the same language as the SBMS itself.

12.3 SUMMARY

Two complimentary structures for supporting software re-use have been presented. The Software Archive serves as a search and retrieval structure for (existing) conventional software in its most general form. Its browsing support leads the user to a component which contains already the highest amount of pre-investment with regard to the current development task. One of the many alternatives in which code might be offered from the Archive is code-contained in a Software Base. This will be an advantageous option in so far, as (re-)specialisation of Software-Base code is foreseen already when it has been written. It is one of the main thrusts of the Software Base concept.

However, there remains one very challenging open problem: There are no metrics for estimating the effort needed to adapt a software component. So far we rely here just on good feeling and even the work on software normalisation (cf.: [7]) is only a very moderate step in this direction.

References

[1] Ben Cherifa A, Mili A, Mittermeir R, Rossak W. A Formal Specification Structure for Software Reuse. TR UBWI 5/89, 1989

[2] Burton BA, Aragon RW, Bailey SA, Koehler KD, Mayes LA. The Reusable Software Library. IEEE Software 1987 4; 4:25-33

[3] Lenz M, Schmid HA, Wolf PF. Software Reuse through Building Blocks. IEEE Software 1987 4; 4:34-42

[4] Mittermeir R. Software Bases for Adaptive Maintenance of Complex Software Systems. In: Proc. of the 7th International ADV-Kongress, Wien, 1983 pp 483-492

[5] Mittermeir R, Oppitz M. Software Bases for the Flexible Composition of Application Systems. IEEE Transactions on Software Engineering 1987 13; 4:157-160

[6] Mittermeir R, Rossak W. Software-Bases and Software-Archives — Alternatives to Support Software Reuse. In: Szygenda S. (chair) Proceedings of the Fall Joint Computer Conference FJCC '87; Exploring Technology: Today and Tomorrow, Dallas TX, USA October 1987. IEEE Computer Society Press, 1987 pp 21-28

[7] Mittermeir R. Design-Aspects Supporting Software Reuse. In: Dusink EM, Hall PAV (eds) Software Reuse: the European Approach. Springer, 1991

[8] Rossak W, Mittermeir R. Structuring Software Archives for Reusability. In: Hamza MH. Proceedings of the Fifth International IASTED Symposium on Applied Informatics, Grindelwald, Switzerland, February, 1987. ACTA, Anaheim 1987 pp 157-160

[9] Rossak W. Ein Konzept zur anwendungsunabhängigen Ablage und Suche von Software in einem Modularchiv. PhD Thesis, Techn. Universität Wien, Austria, March 1989

[10] Rossak W. Software Development Reusing Existing Components — The Software Archive. In: Proc. of the IEEE Phoenix Conference on Computers and Communications PCCC '89, Phoenix AZ, USA, March 1989. pp 327-331

[11] Rossak W, Mittermeir R. A DBMS Based Archive for Reusable Software Components. In: Proceedings of the Second International Workshop on Software Engineering and its Applications, Toulouse, France, December 1989. pp 501-516

Chapter 13

Perspectives of Software Re-usability

K. Sikkel
J.C. van Vliet

13.1 AN INTERDISCIPLINARY APPROACH

"Software Re-usability" is an objective, rather than a field. It emerged as an issue within software engineering, not because of its appeal as a scientific issue per se, but driven by the expected gain in software development productivity.

A comprehensive study of Software Re-usability would be truly interdisciplinary, involving sub-disciplines from computer science, psychology, sociology and anthropology. A software component should be easy to integrate and understandable to the programmer. But that is not enough. How and why do programmers work the way they do? The "not invented here" syndrome is often mentioned as an obstacle to software re-use. But what do we really know about the "programming culture"? In software engineering circles, there is a fair share of folklore, much less knowledge based on scientific investigation, notwithstanding the fact that quite a number of studies addressing programming and design activities (see, eg., [14], [10]) have been done since the early anecdotal stories from [15].

Similarly, the software design process is poorly understood. Eventually, the design phase results in some set of interconnected components. As for these components and their interaction, we are being told to strive for a problem decomposition exhibiting such desirable properties as low coupling and high cohesion. We know little about how to measure these qualities, let alone how to achieve them. Software design is considered to be a trial and error process, where superior performance is achieved by the best people [4].

There is as of yet no theoretical basis for software re-use. The basic issues can only be understood through trial and error. Knowledge about successful and failed re-use attempts is necessary to develop such an understanding. One way to go about is a more anthropological type of research, studying the behaviour of programmers and software designers in the way one studies the behaviour of a specific cultural group. In Software Engineering, this is called an "ecological approach" [1].

The technical aspects of Software Re-usability are overemphasised.

Software Re-usability is an interdisciplinary field — if it is a field at all. Yet, currently, Software Re-usability is a sub-discipline of Software Engineering, which is treated as a technical science at most research institutes. We Software Engineers want to design systems and to build tools. Consequently, if we address Re-usability, we produce prototype re-use systems and tools.

Currently, a variety of languages offers acceptable generics and inheritance features. Information hiding and abstract data types have been known for over a decade. Database and information retrieval techniques offer — perhaps not optimal but surely feasible — means to store and retrieve software components. The semantics of components can be made perfectly clear using formal specification techniques. That is not the problem. The central question is: "what kind of components do we need?". What makes one component better usable than another, and both of them not as usable as we would like them to be?

Many technical aspects of the concept "usable" are known, and have been known for a long time. A more interesting question is "how should I specify a component in such a way that the potential user (ie. the programmer) can easily understand its semantics?" It has been remarked [3] that usability of components is related to their *perceived complexity*. By applying well-known software engineering techniques like data abstraction, information hiding and the provision of small interfaces, the potential re-user can be relieved from the need to have intimate knowledge of implementation details. An equally important aspect, though, concerns the fit between the functionality needed and the functionality offered, and the way such can be ascertained.

Design is very much influenced by experience. Expert designers have a vast body of knowledge that they draw upon. Simon estimates that an expert may have over 50.000 chunks of domain-specific knowledge at his disposal [13]. In human memory, these knowledge chunks form a richly intertwined network. To some extent, software design amounts to mapping the problem at hand to the set of knowledge chunks the designer masters.

This knowledge seems to be invoked through some sort of label identifying the corresponding chunk. If the word "quicksort" rings a bell, we may be able to successfully use a component carrying that name, even if we are not able to reconstruct the corresponding algorithm. At some level, it is a primitive and useful notion whose semantics is well-understood and mutual between different persons using that same notion.

If we believe these non-technical aspects to be important, we should pay them attention and investigate how programmers and designers create mental models of software components. Cognitive issues should be addressed by, or in cooperation with, cognitive scientists.

There is a bright future for research into the field of Human-Computer Interaction. Though numerous widgets exist, most progress is in discovering the real issues that have to be addressed, not in providing definite answers [9]. The field of Programmer-Component Interaction is still much less developed, because the Software Re-usability research community at large fails to address the cognitive issues involved.

The concept "usability" cannot be treated in isolation. Usability only makes sense in relation with a purpose and a user.

It is generally accepted that re-usable software is domain-dependent. It is hard enough to develop components that are generally usable within a specific domain, re-using components from a different domain will clearly be harder. Not only do different domains call for different components, the linguistic framework used to express and communicate their semantics is also different.

From the above discussion it follows that it is easier to use a component when the programmer is familiar with the application domain and easiest when she is familiar with the component as well.

It is in fact much more important to have programmers familiar with the application domain than to have the right set of re-usable components.

13.2 USABLE COMPONENTS ARE HARD TO FIND

We expect that, in general, the usability of components can be increased, and the perceived complexity decreased, when components match primitive concepts of the application domain. In [11] we propose Domain-Oriented Virtual Machines — ie. collections of components that cover the primitives of a particular application domain — as a promising approach to re-usability. The definition of a DOVM is by necessity an iterative process, because there is always a variety of ways in which the domain primitives can be formalised, and there is no way to guarantee that the first attempt is the right one. It may happen, as in [12], that during the first iteration the scope of the domain is not even clear.

Domain analysis is not enough. For the production of truly re-usable components, one needs either a stroke of brilliant insight or a lot of domain experience.

A good domain analysis is one of the hardest tasks there is, and is best carried out by people who are intimately familiar with the domain [8]. To have a domain analysis carried out by people inexperienced with the domain is a guarantee for failure.

Everybody can write a set of components that cover a specific domain. But it is extremely difficult to do it well [5], [2]. If it takes two weeks to design a component, it takes four months to make a truly re-usable component.

Usable software components are pieces of crystallised knowledge.

A really good component is to be valued, not for the trivial reason that it relieves you from implementing its functionality yourself, but for offering you a piece of the right domain analysis, the very functionality you need, gained through much experience and an obsessive desire to find the right abstractions.

Organised software re-use is only possible in sufficiently mature domains.

Application domains have a life cycle of their own. In a new domain, abstractions are highly unstable and software is often written from scratch. Only after a certain period of time, the domain concepts stabilise, software design in the domain becomes more and more standardised. Stabilisation and standardisation come about, preferably when one particular approach emerges as clearly superior, but sometimes because of commercial, political or other external reasons. If one company, system or product dominates its market, it becomes a de facto standard.

When a domain is not yet mature, re-use will necessarily have to be ad hoc. Only after certain standardisation of a domain has taken place, organised forms of re-use in the domain can be expected to be successful.

From this point of view we should even be hesitant to force organised re-use in a domain that has not yet reached maturity through an evolutionary process. Standardisation of components and the corresponding formalisation of domain concepts have a solidifying impact on the primitive notions of a domain. Our notion of these primitives changes because we do not consider them any more as coming from the intuitive universe of discourse, but as being based on the underlying formalism. A crucial question, namely whether we formalised the *right* semantic primitives, then becomes harder to answer.

In some domains, a last step in the life cycle occurs when software re-use itself has been standardised. If standard components are fitted into standard architectures, the re-use process itself can be automated. This is done using application generators or higher-level languages.

A fully automated domain ceases to be a domain, because programming is done at higher levels of abstraction. Programming in third generation languages, for example, has been called "automatic programming" in a distant past. You didn't have to write programs in assembler, the compiler did that for you.

13.3   PERSPECTIVES

So far for the Quest for Perfect Components. The only thing we know for sure is that it's very hard to find them. Yet the more practical problem is that we don't want to wait until the Perfect Components have been uncovered by magic or wizardry.

If we take a pragmatic approach to Software Re-usability, we have to admit that components are not perfect, concepts are never quite standardised, domains keep changing, and hence re-use will at best make a modest contribution to a productivity increase.

Software Re-use quota of 25 % can be realised in industry without any further scientific effort [6], [7]. All the current research into Software Re-usability will not substantially increase this figure before the turn of the century.

A deeper understanding of the re-use problem will not solve the problem. But it will contribute to a better understanding of the software development process as a whole.

Research into Software Re-usability as a means to substantially increase the software productivity will be a rather unsatisfying effort, with at best very limited success. We should look at it from another angle.

If Software Re-usability is to be taken serious as a field of research, it should not primarily aim at increased re-use in the short run, much less concentrate on widgets and paraphernalia of re-use systems, but dig deeper into the real problem. As we have argued above, this is an interdisciplinary matter.

An alternative solution is to turn the subject inside-out. Re-usability isn't a field at all, but there are many different areas of software engineering in which re-usability aspects can be taken into account.

In both cases, the purpose is not re-use. The purpose is to acquire a better understanding of the software development process as a whole. In the long run, this is the only promising approach towards substantial improvements in the quality of software development.

References

[1] Communications of the ACM, special section on Ecological Studies of Professional Programmers, 1988 31; 11:1256-1298

[2] Batory DS, Barnett JR, Roy J, Twichell BC, Garza J. Construction of File Management Systems from Software Components. In: Proc. COMPSAC, Orlando Florida, 1989. pp 358-364

[3] Bott MF, Wallis PJL. Ada and Software Re-Use. Software Engineering Journal 1988 3; 5:574-588

[4] Brooks Jr.FP. No Silver Bullet: Essence and Accidents of Software Engineering. IEEE Computer 1988 20; 4:10-20

[5] Johnson RE, Foote B. Designing Reusable Classes. Journal of Object-Oriented Programming 1988 1; 2:22-30,35

[6] Lanergan RG, Grasso CA. Software Engineering with Reusable Designs and Code. IEEE Transactions on Software Engineering 1984 10; 5:498-501

[7] Matsumoto Y, Management of Industrial Software Production. IEEE Computer 1984 17; 2:59-72

[8] Neighbors JM. The Draco Approach to Constructing Software from Reusable Components. IEEE Transactions on Software Engineering 1984 10; 5:564-574

[9] Norman DA, Draper SW. User Centered System Design. Lawrence Erlbaum Associates, Hillsdale NJ, 1986

[10] Olsen G, Sheppard S, Soloway E. (eds) Empirical Studies of Programmers, Second Workshop. Ablex, Norwood NJ, 1987 In: Olsen GM, Sheppard S, Soloway E. (eds) Empirical Studies of Programmers, Second Workshop, Ablex, Norwood NJ, 1987

[11] Sikkel K, van Vliet JC. Growing Pains of Software Reuse. In: de Ridder ThF. Proceedings Conference Software Engineering in the Nineties 1. Software Engineering Research Centrum, Utrecht, 1988

[12] Sikkel K. A Domain-Oriented Virtual Machine for Control Theory Graphics. Report RP/sre-89/6, Software Engineering Research Centrum, Utrecht, 1989

[13] Simon HA. Problem Solving and Education. In: Tuma DT, Reif F. (eds) Problem Solving and Education: Issues in Teaching and Research. Lawrence Erlbaum Associates, Hillsdale NJ, 1980

[14] Soloway E, Iyengar S. (eds) Empirical Studies of Programmers. Ablex, Norwood NJ, 1986

[15] Weinberg GM. The Psychology of Computer Programming. Van Nostrand Reinhold, 1971

Chapter 14

Using Formal Transformations to Construct a Component Repository

Martin Ward

14.1 INTRODUCTION

Production of software is costly and error prone and the most important means of production (good programmers) are scarce. Therefore, there exists a need to circumvent this costly manual production process. Analogies from classical engineering suggest that by building up a catalogue of standard components and construction techniques whose characteristics are well documented, can greatly reduce the cost of new construction projects. The bridge builder knows under what conditions a "suspension bridge" is the right approach and has a collection of standard girders, cables, nuts, bolts etc. which she can use in the design. This has lead to the notion of a component repository which will reduce the effort involved in constructing new software.

14.1.1 Current Re-use Technology

The desire to avoid writing the same section of code more than once led to the invention of macros and subroutines. These allow the re-use of common code sequences, but the re-use is confined to a single author, or at most a single project. This is too restricted to bring relief to the industry.

Standard subroutine libraries have proved a more powerful technique. Packages like SSP and SPSS have had high success because they not only relieve the programmer from the drudgery of coding but also (in their limited domain of application) relieve him from the need to develop an algorithm, or to understand in detail the theory behind it. Unfortunately, only limited progress has been made in this area since the early days.

We could conceive of a high-level language as an attempt at re-usable canonical structures which frequently occur in programs, such as looping constructs and methods of procedure call, which have been encapsulated into a single command. In addition, common programming *techniques* such as register allocation, loop strength reduction and other optimisations are carried out automatically by the compiling system. In the case of the GNU C compiler [5] "function in-lining" can be carried out automatically: ie. the distinction between macros and procedures has (for almost all practical cases) been removed. The further extension of this idea is restricted by the perceived need for a compilation to be a totally automatic process.

The module or package concept in languages such as Modula-2 or Ada appears to provide even greater support for re-use. The programmer can define data or procedural abstractions and link code of a reasonably general nature into the code she is writing. However, the module implementations at hand are often incompatible with each other since they have been developed independently. They will also be incompatible with the new product under construction. The difficulties involved in re-writing and patching existing code, without introducing bugs, are often greater than the cost of starting from scratch.

Certain operating system features, such as pipes, have been considered to be a means of supporting re-use [3]. A new system is built by combining existing programs using these features.

A problem with having a large library of modules or components is that for it to be re-used effectively the programmer has to know what is available and what each piece of code does, and must be able to combine them on the source code level without any further support from the system. This becomes extremely difficult as the component library gets larger: but that is just when it is becoming useful. As a result these methods have found their greatest success when they are limited to a narrow domain of programs. A 4GL[1] can be seen as an example of a collection of re-usable modules for a narrow programming domain, together with the means to compose them into new programs. A further problem is that only a minor part of the program development effort is spent on coding: therefore, we want to re-use more than just the code. Development methods, designs and documentation should all be re-usable.

14.1.2   Traditional Development Methods

The traditional development methods can be grouped into four main types:

- The traditional "waterfall" life cycle which starts with a fixed specification and develops it into a finished product through a number of stages.

- Incremental development: in which a small part of the product is implemented and then enhanced as the specification is developed.

- Rapid prototyping: in which a prototype of the main part of the system is developed and analysed and used as the bases for the next in a series of prototypes. The traditional waterfall method has been described as "slow prototyping".

- A combination of the above.

All of these methods can be seen as applications of re-use: the initial work (a specification, a partial implementation or a prototype) is re-used in the later stages. Software maintenance can be seen as the development of enhanced products involving a high degree of re-use of the existing product. However, the re-use is almost invariably restricted to a single project, and is often restricted to code re-use.

We want to extend re-use to cross project boundaries and to extend the base of components which can be re-used to include all the products of development work.

---

[1]4th Generation Language

14.2   THE SOFTWARE REPOSITORY

The idea of constructing new software by composition from a collection of re-usable components is not new and clearly has many attractions. However, it has yet to receive widespread implementation. There appear to be several technical reasons for this (in addition to the managerial issues such as the "Not Invented Here" syndrome):

- The repository must be large enough to contain a useful collection of components, yet each component must be readily accessible.

- The components must be highly reliable since they will (hopefully) be re-used in many applications.

- There must be some means for extracting components from existing code for addition to the archive: writing a complete library of components from scratch would involve a great deal of investment of effort before any return on the investment would be perceived.

- In order to be widely useful, the components should be written to handle the most general cases, this means that programs constructed from components can be much less efficient than programs written from scratch which can exploit regularities in the data.

This paper describes how the theory of program refinements and transformations developed in [7],[8] can be applied to the construction of a repository of usable components from which new software can be constructed. The repository contains code, specifications and techniques as the components, connected by formal and informal links. The formal links record proven knowledge about the components, for example an abstract specification will be connected via a *refinement link* to its implementation, two algorithms for solving the same problem will be connected via a *transformation link* and an implementation of an abstract data type in terms of concrete data types will be recorded as a *reification link*. Informal links will enable keyword searches and will connect informal text descriptions of components to other components.

14.3   THEORETICAL FOUNDATION

In [7],[8],[6] a formal theory is developed in which it is possible to prove that one program or specification is a refinement or transformation of another (we define a transformation to be a refinement which works in both directions). The language which is developed along with the theory includes both general specifications (expressed in terms of set theory and first order logic) and standard programming constructs; hence in the following a "program" can be either a program, or a specification, or a hybrid mixture of program and specification (such as a partially-implemented program). A refinement of a program is another program which is more defined (ie. is defined on a larger initial set of states) and more deterministic (ie. for each initial state it has a smaller set of potential final states).

The *semantics* of a program is a mathematical object which captures the external behaviour of the program while ignoring its internal details. In [8] we define the

140

semantics of a program to be a pair $\langle d, r \rangle$ where d is the set of initial states for which the program is *defined* and r is a relation which maps defined initial states to potential final states (we define a *state* to be a finite non-empty collection of variables with values assigned to them). If s and t are states such that $\langle s, t \rangle \in r$, ie. s and t are related under r, then t is a possible final state for the initial state s. In other words, if we start the program in a state in $s \in d$, then it is guaranteed to terminate and the set of possible final states is the set of all states related to s by r. We write $r(s)$ for this set of states, ie.:

$$r(s) = \{t \mid \langle s, t \rangle \in r\} \tag{14.1}$$

If $\langle d_1, r_1 \rangle$ and $\langle d_2, r_2 \rangle$ define the semantics of two programs S_1 and S_2, then we say S_2 refines S_1 iff

$$(d_1 \subseteq d_2) \wedge \forall s \in d_1.(r_2(s) \subseteq r_1(s)) \tag{14.2}$$

If S_1 refines S_2 and S_2 refines S_1 then we say S_1 and S_2 are equivalent. See [8] for the details.

14.3.1 Weakest Preconditions

We use first order logic to express conditions on states, for example the formula $x \geq y$ expresses the condition that the value of the variable x in the state is greater than or equal to that of y. So a formula is either "true" or "false" for a given state: ie. each formula defines a function from the set of states on a given finite non-empty set of variables, to the set of *truth values*, {tt, ff} with the obvious interpretation.

The weakest precondition was introduced by Dijkstra in [2]. For a given program S and condition on the final state (expressed as a formula) R, the weakest precondition $WP(S,R)$ is defined as the weakest condition on the initial state such that starting the program in a state satisfying that condition, results in the program terminating in a final state satisfying the given postcondition. For example, the statement $x := 5$ will terminate in a state satisfying $x > y$ iff it is started in a state satisfying $5 > y$, hence: $WP(x := 5, x > y) = 5 > y$. In [7],[8] we develop a Wide Spectrum Language (WSL) which includes general specifications expressed in first order logic, and imperative programming constructs. We show that the weakest precondition of any program in WSL for any condition on the final state can be expressed as a simple formula of infinitary logic. The infinitary logic we use is a simple extension of standard first order logic which allows the conjunction or disjunction of a countably infinite sequence of formulae as a valid formula. We then go on to prove that the refinement relation between two programs is captured by the implication of their corresponding weakest preconditions, ie. if S_1 and S_2 are programs, then:

$$S_1 \leq S_2 \iff WP(S_1, R) \Rightarrow WP(S_2, R) \tag{14.3}$$

for an arbitrary formula R. This means that the problem of proving a refinement or equivalence on two programs is reduced to proving an implication or equivalence of two formulae, for which all the tools of mathematics are available to assist. This technique has proved highly successful, we have developed a large catalogue of useful transformations and have been able to tackle a diverse range of algorithms and specifications [7],[8],[6].

14.3.2   The Atomic Specification

We want the language we are modeling to include general specifications (expressed in terms of mathematical logic) as well as programs. This will reduce the task of proving that a program is a correct implementation of a specification to one of proving that one statement (the program) is a refinement of another statement (the specification). Instead of having two languages (a specification language and a programming language) all our proofs are carried out within a single *wide spectrum language*. When implementing specifications as executable programs, we will often need to assign values to temporary variables which are not mentioned in the specification and whose final values do not matter. To express this, we need a notation for adding and removing variables from the set of active variables (called the "state space"). Both of these concepts are combined in a new primitive statement, the *atomic specification* which specifies a program using logical formulae:

Definition 1 *The Atomic Specification:* written $\mathbf{x}/\mathbf{y}.\mathbf{Q}$, where $\mathbf{Q}$ is a formula of first order logic and $\mathbf{x}$ and $\mathbf{y}$ are sequences of variables, is a form of nondeterministic assignment statement. Its effect is to add the variables in $\mathbf{x}$ to the state space, assign new values to them such that $\mathbf{Q}$ is satisfied, remove the variables in $\mathbf{y}$ from the state and terminate. If there is no assignment to the variables in $\mathbf{x}$ which satisfies $\mathbf{Q}$, then the Atomic Specification does not terminate (ie. it is not defined for those initial states).

This is based on the "atomic description" of Back [1].

Some examples of Atomic Specifications:

1. $\langle x \rangle / \langle \rangle.(x > y)$ This sets x to any value greater than the value of y. If there is no such value, then the specification does not terminate.

2. $\langle z \rangle / \langle \rangle.(z = x + y); \langle \rangle / \langle z \rangle.(x = z)$ This sequence implements the assignment statement $x := x + y$, using a temporary variable z.

3. $\mathbf{x\prime}/.\mathbf{Q}; \mathbf{x}/\mathbf{x\prime}.(\mathbf{x} = \mathbf{x\prime})$ Here $\mathbf{x}$ is a sequence of variables and $\mathbf{x\prime}$ a sequence of temporary variables. These statements implement the general assignment statement: $\mathbf{x} := \mathbf{x\prime}.\mathbf{Q}$, which assigns new values $\mathbf{x\prime}$ to $\mathbf{x}$ where $\mathbf{Q}$ gives the relation between $\mathbf{x}$ and $\mathbf{x\prime}$.

4. $\langle n, x, y, z \rangle / \langle \rangle.(n, x, y, z \in N^+ \wedge (n > 2) \wedge (z^n = x^n + y^n))$ This example illustrates the fact that proving the termination of even a single primitive statement of WSL can be quite a challenge!

14.3.3   The Join Construct

Together with the atomic description and more familiar programming constructs, the Wide Spectrum Language includes a new construct called *join*. The join of two programs is defined to be the weakest (ie. least defined) program which satisfies any specification satisfied by either of the two programs. If one of the component programs does not terminate for a particular initial state, then it cannot satisfy any specification defined on that state, so the join of the two programs is identical to the other program on that state. A property of the join construct is that any program which refines both components will also refine their join. This property is very useful in searching the repository: if we have a specification which we wish to implement, we first want to search the database for an equivalent (or at least similar) specification which has already been implemented. For a large and complex specification this will give rise to a potentially highly complex matching problem. If, however, the specification is expressed as the join of several simpler specifications, then the matching problem for each component will be much easier to solve. Once we have found all the components, we can search through the refinement links to find a common ancestor to all of the components. From the above property of join, this ancestor will be a correct implementation of the full specification. We give an example of this search below.

We have used this theory to develop tools for the development of algorithms and programs from specifications, and the derivation of specifications from code (we term this process "inverse engineering"). A large catalogue of practical transformations and refinements has been developed which are being applied to a wide variety of programs.

14.4 WHY INVENT *ANOTHER* NEW LANGUAGE?

There are several reasons why we have invented another language rather than using an existing programming language such as C or Ada:

- We needed a language with a simple semantics and tractable reasoning methods. In particular, our language has been designed from the start with ease of transformation and refinement as a major objective. New constructs are added to the language only if we can show that they will be easy to work with: in particular, we need a useful set of transformations which make use of that construct before it becomes part of the language. This policy has proved very successful and enabled us to avoid some of the problems which can occur when the language definition is the starting point for research.

- We wanted to include the implementation of a (possibly non-executable) specification as an allowable refinement step, we also wanted to be able to write programs using a mixture of specification and programming constructs. This facilitates the stepwise refinement of specifications into programs and the iterative analysis of programs into specifications. No existing implementable programming language includes general specifications in its syntax (for obvious reasons!).

- By expressing our results in a general language, we get results which are independent of any particular programming language. Programs in existing programming language can be transcribed into WSL, manipulated as WSL programs, and then re-transcribed, perhaps into a different programming language.

- All existing programming languages have limitations (in particular, the limitation to executable constructs which is intolerable in a specification language). Also many popular languages have a number of quirks and foibles which would greatly complicate the semantics while adding little expressive power.

14.5 COMPONENTS

The components in out repository will consist of pieces of Wide Spectrum Language (WSL) code [7],[8]: this code could be either a program module or the specification of a module, or a mixture of programming constructs and specifications. We have extended the WSL language to express metaprogramming constructs (ie. program editing operations, transformations and refinements). This means that as well as recording the specification and implementation of a module as two components, the sequence of transformations used to derive the implementation from the specification can also be recorded as a third component. These derivation histories can be generalised into derivation *strategies* which can also be transformed by applying metatransformations written in a meta-meta-programming language. In fact, the meta-meta-programming language is identical with the metaprogramming language, since this is simply an extension of WSL.

Documentation and informal requirements in the form of text are also included as components of the repository.

14.6 COMPONENT LINKS

The components are connected together, using links to form the repository; there are two different types of link:

Formal links which record proven facts about the components and which are, therefore, transitive. These are of four different types:

1. **Change in data representation:** $\longrightarrow$ This links two programs which are equivalent in effect, but which use different representations of the data.

2. **Refinement:** $\longrightarrow$ This links a "less defined" program to a refinement of it.

3. **Transformation:** $\overset{\longleftarrow}{\longrightarrow}$ This links two programs which are equivalent, but which may use different internal data or algorithms for example.

4. **Reification:** $\overset{\cong}{\longrightarrow}$ This is similar to transformation in that it links equivalent programs, but the program to the right uses a less abstract internal data representation and less abstract algorithms and is, therefore, closer to an implementation.

Informal links: $\cdots\cdots\blacktriangleright$ These connect documentation, informal requirements and keywords to the other components.

14.7 AN EXAMPLE

In this section we present a small example of a fragment of a repository concerning sorting programs. For the moment we will restrict attention to a subset of the repository components and the formal links which connect them. The components are as follows (here $A[1..n]$ is an array of elements to be sorted in place):

- **abort**: this is the totally undefined program, any program is, therefore, a refinement of **abort**.

- *random_perm* = $A := A\prime.(\exists \pi \in Perms(n).\forall 1 \leq i \geq n.A[\pi(i)] = A\prime[i])$: here *Perms(n)* is the set of all permutations of the elements $\{1, ..., n\}$. This program nondeterministically permutes the elements of array A.

- *random_inc_seq* = $\langle A \rangle / \langle \rangle.Sorted(A)$: here $Sorted(A) =_{df} \forall 1 \leq i < j \leq n.A[i] \leq A[j])$ ie. it is true iff array A is sorted. This program assigns arbitrary values to the array such that it is sorted.

- *SORT* = **join** *random_inc_seq* $\sqcap$ *random_perm* **nioj** : This is a specification of a program to sort A. Note that it gives no indication of the algorithm to use (testing all possible assignments of increasing sequences to see which are permutations of the original array is not a practical sorting algorithm!). Note the use of **join** to split up the specification into two simpler subspecifications. (Sort is probably a simple enough concept by itself — this is just an example to illustrate the technique).

- *merge_sort_array*: this is the implementation of a merge sorting algorithm.

- *merge_sort_file*: this is obtained from *merge_sort_array* by changing the data representation: we use an array to represent a file.

- *recursive_quicksort*: this is obtained from *SORT* by "algorithm derivation" (see below).

- *iterative_quicksort*: a reified algorithm obtained from *recursive_quicksort*.

- *Ada_quicksort*: obtained from *iterative_quicksort* by transforming into a form which can be automatically translated into an efficient Ada module.

- *C_quicksort*: see *Ada_quicksort*.

The links which connect these components are shown diagrammatically in figure 14.1. Let us suppose that the user of the repository wishes to implement a sorting algorithm. He writes his specification in the form of a **join** of smaller specifications with which he then searches the repository to see if implementations already exist. The initial stages of the search could make use of informal

links: for instance an analysis of the specifications would suggest that "Array" would be a suitable keyword to restrict the search to specifications of array manipulation programs. Theorem-proving techniques can be applied to prove, for instance, that *random_perm* is a refinement of one component of the specification, and that *random_inc_seq* is a refinement of the other component. Once refinements of all components have been found, then the refinement and reification links can be searched automatically to find a common descendant of all the refinements. In this case *SORT* will be found immediately.

Note that the process of finding a common ancestor could fail: for example, the system might notice that **skip** is a refinement of *random_perm*, but the **join** of **skip** and *random_inc_seq* is not fully defined (in fact it is the guard $[Sorted(A)]$. If a guard or other partially-domained statement (or "miracle" as some authors refer

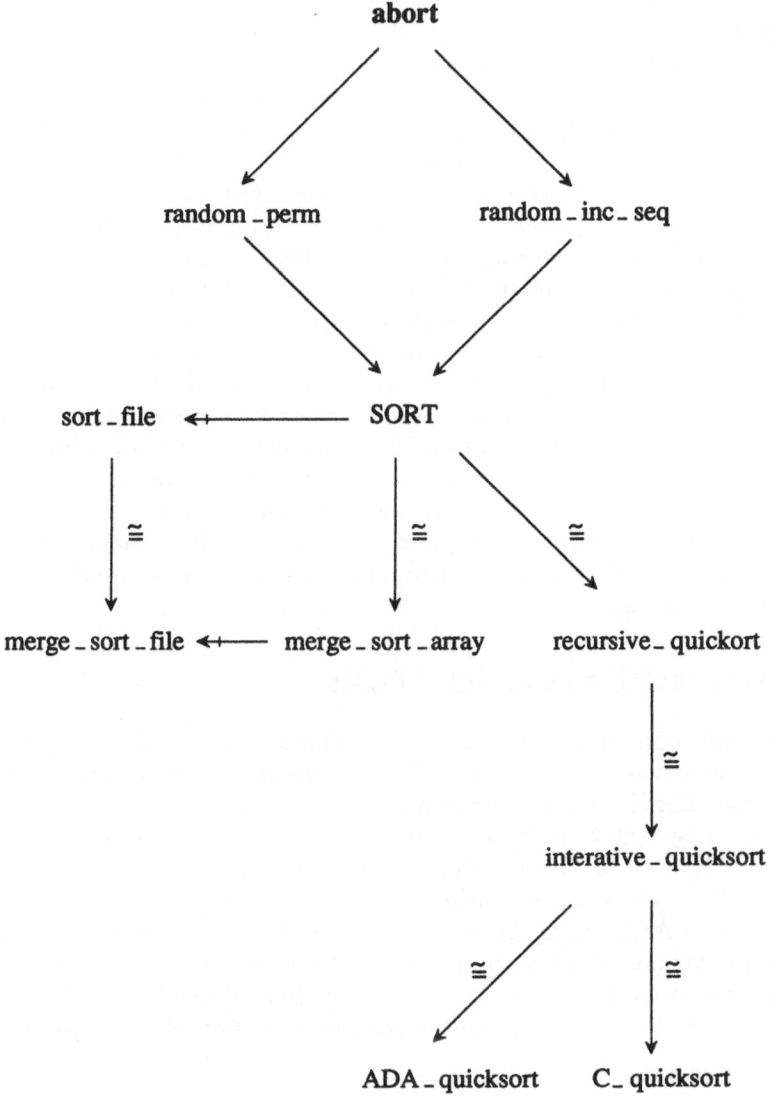

Figure 14.1 A Fragment of a Repository

to it, for example [4]) is reached in the search for a common descendant, then the search has failed since such a specification cannot be implemented.

Once *SORT* has been found, the various implementations of the specification can be extracted by following the reification links. For example, the "quicksort" implementation could be selected. This has previously been transformed into an efficient iterative algorithm which has been massaged into two forms; one appropriate for translation to C and the other for Ada. See [10] for the derivation of the programs from the *SORT* specification. Alternatively a file sorting algorithm could be extracted by following the "change data representation" links.

This process is analogous to the process we go through when selecting a purchase from the set of manufacturer's offerings. We have a rough idea of what we want, which is still precise enough for us to check it against the given supply. Our requirements are frequently expressed as a set of objectives which we require to be simultaneously achieved. (This is analogous to writing a specification as the join of a set of incomplete specifications. A suitable implementation has to satisfy all the component specifications). As we narrow down the set of possibilities, we add more details to our specification and make more precise discriminations. If no ready-built product is suitable, then we may choose to get one specially manufactured; the manufacturing process will throw up requirements for components which will have to be searched for in turn.

14.8 ADDING EXISTING CODE

One problem with current research on re-use is that several people have produced prototype component repositories, but nobody wants to start using them because of the enormous effort involved in developing a large enough set of components for the repository to be useful. With the system presented here this problem is much less acute: existing code can be placed in the repository, initially with informal links only. Later, as the code is analysed using code analysis and specification tools such as the Maintainer's Assistant [6],[9]. This process can be carried out in conjunction with normal maintenance; as the specifications of code are extracted, they can be placed in the repository. In addition the transformational development of new code from specifications and components will provide new components and links for the repository.

14.9 PROBLEMS AND BENEFITS

14.9.1 Problems

- **Specification Matching:** Any repository or component library is only as good as the technique for matching specifications and extracting components. This is a difficult problem in general: the problem gets more difficult as the library gets larger, but this is just when it is becoming more useful. We believe that the technique of including a large collection of "partial" or "generic" specifications, which can be composed using the **join** operator, will greatly assist in finding the required component and eliminating unsuitable matches. With a large set of generics there will be a number of paths through the repository, from the results of an initial informal keyword browse to the desired component. Thus the large size of the library actually *assists* in the search rather than hindering it. Developing a "standard style" for writing specifications and a standard set of generics for composing larger specifications will greatly assist the theorem proving specification matcher and improve the ease with which specifications and other components can be extracted.

- **Size of Repository:** The more components and links (especially formal links) there are in the repository, the more useful it will be in the construction of new software. Many of the components will be substantial pieces of code or documentation, including perhaps many different versions of the same piece of code tailored for different purposes. Thus the overall size of the repository is likely to be very large. This can be alleviated with the use of optical WORM[2] storage, since most of the operations will consist of reading from and adding to the repository with only very occasional deletions.

- **Efficiency:** Constructing a program from a set of general-purpose re-usable components can often generate a highly inefficient result. There may be extra layers of procedure calls plus the general-purpose modules are not able to make use of regularities in the data for the current program to carry out their actions more efficiently. This problem can be avoided by the application of *efficiency improving transformations* to the generated code. Optimising compilers carry this out at a very low level: they construct the program from standard code blocks which implement the high-level constructs and then optimise the result to try and remove the inefficiencies introduced. The transformations we have developed work at a higher level than any optimising compiler, they include removing unnecessary procedure calls, migrating code between modules, adding data structures to store intermediate results rather than re-calculating, changing the representation of data structures, etc. Because the transformations have been proven to preserve the effect of the program, and because they can be applied and the correctness conditions checked automatically, there is no chance of introducing clerical or logical errors in a long series of transformations. Hence they can be used freely wherever appropriate to improve the efficiency of the final product to a sufficient degree. The resulting modules can in turn be added to the repository and re-used, as can any new efficiency improving techniques which are developed.

14.9.2 Benefits

- Recording formal as well as informal links in the repository means that the work involved in proving that a module correctly implements its specification is not lost, but is repaid many times over.

- The repository records specifications and development methods as well as code, so these can be re-used in the same way.

- Maintenance work carried out using tools such as the "Maintainer's Assistant" [9] generates new components with validated high-level specifications as a by-

---

[2]Write Once Read Many

product. These can be incorporated in the repository, so that the existing development and maintenance investment can be made greater use of.

- The creation of formal links means that there is a high degree of confidence that the components in the repository meet their specifications, hence new programs constructed from these components will be correspondingly reliable.

- The efficiency improving transformations make it possible to construct efficient programs out of general purpose components.

- The derivation of specifications from old code undergoing maintenance means that such code can be brought into a CASE strategy.

14.10   CONCLUSION

We have described a theory for program transformation and refinement which has proved very powerful for the derivation of programs from specifications and the analysis of existing programs in software maintenance [9]. This, together with the join concept for composing specifications and programs, and the "metaprogramming" language for describing program developments, forms the foundation for the construction of a repository of re-usable components which can be used in the construction of new software with greater reliability at greatly reduced cost.

References

[1] Back RJR. Correctness Preserving Program Refinements. Mathematisch Centrum, Mathematical Centre Tracts 131, 1980

[2] Dijkstra EW. A Discipline of Programming. Prentice-Hall, Englewood Cliffs, NJ, 1976

[3] Kernighan BW. The UNIX System and Software Reusability. IEEE Transactions on Software Engineering 1984 10; 5:513-528

[4] Morgan CC. The Specification Statement. ACM TOPLAS 1988 10; :403-419

[5] Stallman RM. Using and Porting GNU CC. Free Software Foundation, Inc., 1989

[6] Ward M. Transforming a Program into a Specification. Durham University, Technical Report 88/1, 1988

[7] Ward M. Proving Program Refinements and Transformations. PhD Thesis, University of Oxford, 1989

[8] Ward M. A Model for Partial Programs. Submitted to Journal of the ACM, 1989;

[9] Ward M, Calliss FW, Munro M. The Maintainer's Assistant. Conference on Software Maintenance 1989, Miami Florida, 1989

[10] Ward M. Derivations of Sorting Algorithms. Forthcoming, 1990

References

Author Index